ISBN (ebk): 978-1-7380107-1-4
ISBN (pbk): 978-1-7380107-0-7

Front cover image and book design by Sheldon Bailey

First printing edition 2023

Dedication

This book is dedicated to my wife, Sophon.

A supportive friend and a devoted spouse, she came into my life at precisely the right time and has changed my view about what is and isn't possible for myself. This book and my place in life would never have materialized if she wasn't in my life and I am grateful for that.

Acknowledgements

I would like to acknowledge my family – my wife Sophon and children (Shereece, Samantha, Shemar and Sheldon Jr.) for allowing me the time and space to achieve this personal goal of authoring a book.

I would also like to acknowledge everyone that was mentioned in this book. You have all had a profound impact in my life and I am truly thankful for the interactions that we've had over the years.

Note: *Pseudonyms are used at some points in the book, indicated by the use of an asterisk (*).*

Table of Contents

Prelude

I haven't lived the most eventful life – not by a long shot. Growing up in a large family that always maintained a humble lifestyle, I was never exposed to some luxuries that others around me were able to enjoy. I played video games when I visited friends, I learned to ride a bike through the kindness of a neighbor, I used to be the remote control for the lone TV in the house, and I was responsible for hand-washing my own laundry by the age of 10. In my tender years, I convinced myself that my whole existence was akin to life within a concentration camp – it was all cruel and unusual punishment to me. That all changed when adulthood hit, even more so when I became a father. All the lessons that my parents taught me without teaching me were suddenly of enormous importance and needed to be passed on to my offspring.

I now recognize that the discipline that is required to handle the daily grind of *adulting* was never passed on to me by instruction but ingrained through tasks and experience. Who I am today is mostly attributable to the lessons received from my parents, most of which were never offered formally. I am now out of my parents' house and have a unit of my own that bears my last name. Still, the life-long learner in me continues to believe in the learning opportunities that are constantly provided through everyday happenings.

In this book I recount a small number of pivotal learning moments that I have encountered over the course of my life so far. There are many, many more that I could easily refer to, but I don't think it would be appropriate to bombard the world with all 9 of the encyclopedia-like volumes it would take to document those. Instead, I choose to pull on experiences that have occurred at different points in my life – different kinds of interactions with various types of people – to give a more rounded recount with greater contextual span. Each chapter is composed of a true story from my memory banks, followed by a lesson that may be gleaned from that story. I am fully aware that lessons learned from an experience is wholly subjective and I do not present my learnings as gospel. While the stories are fixed in time, readers may feel free to pull from them what they wish or what applies.

I would encourage you, the reader, to approach the content of this book with the lightness of heart with which it was written, while being careful to embrace the life-changing principles contained in each lesson.

CHAPTER 1

THE ANTICHRIST

As I write this chapter, I am celebrating my 1-week anniversary of passing my level 1 swim class.

Yes, you read that right! This Island boy who spent so many years on a land with a name that stems from an Arawak word meaning "land of Wood and Water" is finally learning how to swim. And this is not due a lack of trying either. My father would take us to the beach regularly, making it his point of duty to take us out into the deep one at a time. I also have many memories of family and church picnics that would see us spending an entire day on a sandy seashore, or on one of the many riverbeds that can be found on the island. My mother even signed me up for swim lessons in my junior high school years, but still, after all of that, I grew into an adult who was as comfortable in water as a fish would be in a coconut tree.

Funnily though, the more I grew and shared my natatorial ineptitude, the more I realized that I wasn't alone. If, for whatever reason, a social conversation should ever veer into the subject of swimming, there would always be at least one other adult confessing their lack of the skill as well. Such declarations would usually evoke a few comments of awe and wonder, trying to understand how it is possible that people could make it to adulthood without being able to challenge Nemo to a race. The reasons that I have heard being given usually boil down to, "I never got the chance to learn" or "it just never happened for me".

My reason was quite simply this: I never learned to swim because I was deathly afraid of drowning. Now you may say, "that is the exact reason to learn to swim", and you would be right. But learning to swim necessitated that I got into the water, and my fear of drowning kept me out of the water. It was a situation that would hold me captive on the beach, river stone, and poolside for decades. My lack of swimming skills was well-known to my peers (who were all swimmers), and I went through many years of jeering due to this. But one of my most memorable aquatic experiences involve these very same friends – friends who [usually] had the best of intentions.

When *Gary began moving up the corporate ranks at his office, one of the perks that came with his progress was an access card to the company's recreational spot. This was a well-appointed piece of real estate that had an indoor gym area, an outdoor pool, and well-manicured lawns that would readily provide the perfect setting for a picnic or a photo shoot. As young men, we would frequent that spot on Sunday afternoons with our special ladies in tow. For some of us, it was a free way to foster some family togetherness, while for others, it was a free way to score some points with the girl whose attention we were trying to arrest at that time. It was on one of these Sunday afternoons that Gary voiced his frustration with seeing me splash about in the shallow end. He had watched me embarrass myself for way too long and he was going to put an end to it. On that day, he was going to teach me how to swim.

Gary was probably the strongest swimmer of us all. Though he was a heavy guy with slightly below-average athletic ability on land, he was a natural in the water. That boy could move like a torpedo without displacing a drop of water. (Ok…fine. I exaggerate. But he was almost that good.)

When he made the announcement that he was going to do what had been deemed impossible by others, there were snickers from the rest of the group. I looked at him and the look in his eyes communicated quite clearly that he wasn't joking. I probably should have firmly declined in that moment but wanting to impress my wife of less than a year, who was present and looking on, clouded my better judgement. There were no lifeguards on duty, no one with formal training in water rescue, and I was probably the only one there who was certified in CPR. The whole situation was a disaster waiting to happen, but before I had my head wrapped around what was going on I found myself clutching to the wall in the deep end of the pool, with Gary standing over me from the safety of the pool deck like a sentinel with a long pole in his right hand. His plan, as it was explained, was brilliant in its simplicity:

> **Step 1:** I push off from the wall and try to keep my head above water by treading. (I think he might have been of the understanding that the definition of 'treading' was common knowledge, and that I was a holder of said knowledge. Little did he know that nothing could have been further from the truth.)
>
> **Step 2:** He was going to keep a close eye on me and give me tips on what to do, and what to do better as we progressed.
>
> **Step 3:** If ever I was to find myself getting in trouble, I was to yell "POLE", and he would stretch the pole towards me.
>
> **Step 4:** I was then to grab that pole and be pulled to safety.

Looking back now, I cannot fathom how I let him talk me into trusting him with my life when he was not even planning on getting into the water, but I did. Everyone was in the shallow end, waiting to see me follow Gary's instructions and go through this apparently necessary rite of passage.

I hung on to the wall for dear life. I tried to let go so many times, but my fingers were much smarter than the rest of my body that day – they refused to unfurl. Finally, after much cheering and jeering, I pushed off the wall, let go, and started sinking almost immediately. I don't even think I was able to engage my arms or my legs into any kind of water support technique before I swallowed my first mouthful of water. I couldn't call for help nor was I able to yell "POLE" like I was supposed to. I was going down like the 150lb boulder that I was. It was reported after the ordeal that Gary had indeed stretched the pole out to me in a desperate attempt to provide the promised assistance, but my eyes were so tightly shut that I couldn't see to grab it even if it was there.

I was in a bad spot. From beneath the surface of the water, I could hear the muffled sounds of panicked shouting and urgent calls for intervention by the onlookers. I tried my best to stay afloat by frantically splashing about, but nothing I was doing was working. There was minor pandemonium but somehow, in the midst of it all, I had an idea - the origin of which befuddles me to this day. I made one last big kick that raised my head just enough for me to take in a big breath, and then I just…..stopped. I stopped kicking, I stopped splashing. I stopped moving my hands. I just stopped. I let myself sink and continue sinking until I hit the bottom of the pool. Once I felt my feet touch the bottom of the pool, I proceeded to walk under the water from the deep end of the pool towards the shallow end where everyone else was gathered. My eyes remained tightly closed, both because of my hatred of getting chlorine in my eyes and because I was deep in concentration. I steadily made my way through what was threatening to be my watery grave, climbing the incline of the pool floor - heading for shallow water.

When I felt my head break the water's surface, I made one last big leap that allowed me to fill my lungs with fresh air. I cannot recall another instance in my life where I was so happy to take a breath! I smiled in triumph and panted with relief. Wiping the water from my face, I opened my eyes and looked around to see everyone staring at me quite quizzically. Apparently, I had done something that was never before thought to be 'a thing'. Within a flash the concerned-but-curious demeanors were replaced with side-busting laughter. The whole episode took a comic turn that segued ever so neatly into the typical lightheartedness of these kinds of gatherings.

For a quite a while after that afternoon I would often be referred to as "the antichrist'. Apparently, it made sense that since Jesus (of the Bible) is the Christ, and there was an occasion where He walked on water, then I, having walked under water, must be the antichrist.

Sigh….

Being able to maintain a sense of control during times of adversity is an underrated, but extremely important skill. In the midst of turmoil and strife, it is often very difficult to envision an end to the struggle or imagine any kind of triumph that is to follow the battle being faced. But what I have found to be true is that the nature or intensity of any challenge will have as much effect as it is allowed to. Though tempting, finding oneself in a tough spot is never reason enough to call it quits or to throw one's hands in the air.

To this day, I find that facing seemingly insurmountable challenges brings me back to that Sunday afternoon in the pool where I symbolically re-enact the sequence of events from that day - a re-enactment that I will share (in principle) here:

1. **Take a breath:** Fight for it if you must! That *breath* is needed to sustain you as you face the challenge at hand. There are times when adverse situations can be seen coming, while other times they will appear without warning. Whether taken by surprise or not, find that moment in time where there is the possibility for taking a breath. That *breath* could be anything that keeps your purpose in view. It may be memories of previous battles won, or of family members that are counting on you. It could also be, as dark as it sounds, the desire to prove to naysayers that they were wrong about you. Whatever the breath is for you, take it in! Breathe deeply! Fill your lungs with the 'air' that you need to carry on and hold on to it.

2. **Don't panic - use your energy wisely:** As much as you want to, and as natural as the tendency may feel, giving into panic is the most certain way to remain in the challenge and sink deeper into despair. Kicking and thrashing about are other natural responses to desperate circumstances, but rarely do they produce a desired result. Let those that are looking on do the panicking for you. Being in the "*water*", provides a vantage point that no one else has. There is an intimate acquaintance with the challenge that those who are looking on are left to imagine, deduce, or conjure up some identity for. Being mindful of

where you are and what it is that you face, but keeping your emotions and imagination in check will allow for the maintenance of control. Panic clouds the mind and negatively impacts its ability to process anything in a systematic (and ultimately useful) way.

3. **Get to work:** The approach taken in this step will vary based on the nature of what is being dealt with, but I have found that it is often more effective to work through a challenge than to work around it. This is a sentiment that is often debated, as there are some who see 'a workaround' as the smarter approach due to the apparent ease that it offers. I do agree with that component of the argument – a workaround is often easier, but real and lasting success is usually born from the former. While maintaining a focus on the desired end, each step taken must be measured and intentional – moving towards that destination. Limit the amount of time spent dawdling or grieving your circumstance and make good use of that life-saving breath taken earlier, the breath that is sustaining the journey. Make every effort to work towards the goal – not away from it.

To date, I have found that some journeys have been longer than others, and some waters have proven to be deeper than previously experienced. But up until right now, I am yet to come upon an instance where my three-step approach has left me stranded. The shallow end of the pool ALWAYS comes.

Not every troubling situation will present the same threat as the deep end of a swimming pool to a non swimmer - some troubles are worse than others. Nevertheless, the sad truth is that life-altering troubles are guaranteed to everyone as they make their journey around the sun. The question is never if, but when. On that day when the tempests blow and the tides rise, staying afloat is a noble aspiration that should be pursued. But should you find yourself sinking in one of the very bad storms, remember that sinking is not the end, nor is drowning a guaranteed outcome of sinking. Drowning is the most likely outcome only when one sinks without a plan.

"Even though I walk through the darkest valley, I will fear no evil, for you are with me.." - Psalm 23:4

CHAPTER 2

BLUE TEDDY

Should you come across this stuffed toy, you, like most others, will see a raggedy old blue teddy bear who has obviously seen better days. Like Rainbow, Pinky-poo, Patrick, Rabbie, and Uni-princess, "Blue Teddy" has become an integral inanimate member of our family and is very likely to be another reason for me being sent back into a burning building to execute a rescue. On most nights Blue Teddy and Rabbie will be found snuggled up between my boys (who insist on sharing a bed), ensuring a peaceful night's sleep for the duo and, by extension, the rest of the house.

Psychology attributes the dependence of stuffed animals to one of the many stages of growth for a child. I am not about to argue how true that sentiment is, but if it is true then it seems I skipped a step in developmental years. I didn't grow up with stuffed toys and I am therefore unenraptured by them. Actually, if I am to be perfectly honest, I did have a little brown monkey puppet as a young boy, but my fondness for him was based more on him being a gift from my favorite Uncle. I was just never much into stuffies and if you ask around in my house even now you will likely hear that I am indifferent to those lifeless creations. Blue Teddy, on the other hand, has a special place in my heart…..

Hailing from a factory far far away in Oakland, New Jersey, Blue Teddy wandered into our lives in the Christmas season of 2019. I was a new international student in Toronto Canada and was just finishing up my first term of my first graduate program. Only 4 months before, I had hugged my wife and kissed my 11-month-old first born as I set off to upskill myself and subsequently position my family for a better future. This being my first trip to Canada, I had landed in Toronto on that frigid Tuesday evening, unsure of what was waiting for me. I was met at the airport by my cousin and her husband, who both got a good chuckle out of seeing the Islander tremble in the 'cold' 21-degree Celsius weather. Their amusement was lost on me at the time – I was freezing! Whenever my native Jamaica had to deal with a cold weather system, it would never get below 27 degrees. So, 21 degrees was numbingly cold for me, from any angle. I learned pretty quickly thereafter that in Canada, 21-degree days are when the tank tops and cut offs come out! But what can I say? I was naïve at the time.

Naïve or not, I was certainly relieved when we got to the dorms and I entered the place that was to be my home for the next academic year. The dorms were quite nice, with each room being single-occupancy and having its own bathroom attached. The kitchen and lounge were common areas, but it was comforting to know that I would have my own space to deal with my bouts of homesickness – which I expected to be a common occurrence. I put on a brave facc, intent on showing the world that I was man enough for the challenge, though I was scared and shaking inside.

But God's favor would soon find its way to me.

The comings and goings of the days following revealed that I had a few classmates who were also living on the dorm. We didn't all end up being friends, but we were all friendly enough to one another. We would go for walks together, go on the odd grocery trip together, and would often gather in front of the big screen TV in the den to watch episodes of *Lost* and *Friends* (not everyone will know what I'm talking about here but for those who know, YOU KNOW!).

There was one guy in particular though – Glenn – he and I just seemed to 'click'.

Glenn was of East Asian descent and just an all-around decent guy. We shared an interest in the guitar and he would lend me his so I could practice from time to time, even though those sessions didn't really amount to anything much for me. If I was having an off evening and didn't feel like being around anyone, I was sure to get a thumb-drive the next day bearing the Episode of *Lost* that I missed. I can honestly say that Glenn had my back, in and out of class!

But as much of a stand-up guy that he was in general, he would soon go on to hit the proverbial ball right out of the park…..

As the Fall term progressed and the temperature began to fall even further (for no good reason whatsoever), the fuzzy feelings that accompany the yuletide season started to come in waves. Evening strolls and window-shopping expeditions at the mall were all becoming painful as I would see families laughing, talking, eating together – a strong reminder of all that I was missing. The side-busting laughter of little kids as they raced around is a sound that is meant to brighten the day of even the most down-trodden. But for me, those laughs were a source of almost-physical pain. Soon the separation became too much. As much as my wife and I barely had two coins to rub together, we managed to amass enough to buy plane tickets for her and our daughter so we could all spend Christmas together in Canada. Interestingly enough, it was cheaper for both of them to visit me in the icebox that is Canada than it was for me to go back to the warm sunshine of home. I roll my eyes those airline folks!

Sophon was in the middle of her first master's program at the time (yes, we tend to be crazy like that) but, luckily, our school break coincided. The day that I bought the tickets marked a countdown that filled me with glee. I guess the excitement was firmly stamped on my face because everyone was asking why I was aglow, and I was not shy to share the news! I was going to have my family with me for Christmas and I was unashamedly stoked! In no time at all I had winter clothes all lined up for both girls, along with extra bedding, bus pass, food, you name it! The Christmas spirit was in the air, and everyone was breathing it in by the tankful.

They landed on Friday night, and I made sure to be at the front of the crowd when passengers from their flight started to come down the ramp after being vetted by the Customs officers. Our daughter, now just over 1 year old, clung to her mother for dear life, trying to get away from this strange man who was reaching out to her. It stung a little, but I understood. We got back to my tiny suite, and, after a welcome supper, they promptly fell asleep. I tried to sleep as well, but I spent most of the night just sitting in the chair, watching them sleep, listening to the snoring and awing at the thumb-sucking. I was finally whole again – if only for two weeks.

By the next morning the ice was broken and my little girl had all but forgotten that she had a mom. She followed me everywhere I went, only eating if I were the one to feed her, seeking my approvals before an action – I was elated!! Mommy grumbled a little, but she got it. After all, she remembered what it was like to be a daddy's girl.

A few gentle but firm knocks on the door interrupted our late-morning breakfast. Through the peephole I saw Glenn. I didn't expect anyone to be around since school was out on break. Everyone should have gone home for the holidays. I soon learned that He was also on his way out to his folks' place but stopped by to drop off something. As we spoke in the doorway, he saw a pair of questioning eyes fixed firmly on him. I watched as he knelt, smiling gently, holding out a little stuffed toy, Blue Teddy, that he had picked up when he heard that my family was coming to visit.

Blue Teddy had found a little mom who loved him more than she loved Dora (which was saying something), and she held on to him for dear life until her prayer for a sibling was answered 7 years later. I teared up a little the day that I watched her pass Blue Teddy on to her baby sister, who would give it to *her* baby brother a few years later.

I keep waiting for the day when that brother decides to keep the tradition going, but it doesn't seem like it's ever going to happen. Blue Teddy is his buddy and that's just the way its gonna be!

This episode in my life comes back to me every time I stand at the shore of a lake or a river, especially if my sons are around. The natural thing to do when visiting a body of water (at least for me and mine) is to throw rocks in. Inevitably, a rock entering said body of water will create a splash on entry and that truth remains regardless of the size of the rock. A boulder will produce a huge splash while a pebble will create a little splash, but one way or another, a splash follows the tossing of the rock. My little ones are most fond of the sudden disruption of the calm waters when they toss the rock, so much so that their ongoing competition is to see who can find and toss the largest one (makes me nervous every time). My favorite part of the action, however, is to observe the ripples that emanate in all directions from the point of impact. Those ripples can travel great distances across the water's surface if left unencumbered or uninterrupted. The distance that they travel is also reflective of the size of the initial disruptive event, meaning ripples from larger rocks travel further out than those from smaller rocks.

Blue Teddy created a ripple effect in my family not once, but 3 different times. His warmth, security, and companionship has been felt repeatedly. Every time that he changes hands is akin to a new splash being made in my family pond with the ripples being reinvented and renewed. The giver is rewarded by the satisfaction of sharing and giving, while the receiver gets to be touched by life-changing kindness.

The human community needs more of these splashes of kindness! The emphasis being placed on 'kindness' here is intentional because the ripple effect is not constrained to positive interactions. In much the same way that a kind act can travel through time and across generations, so can acts of injustice and evil. It is not difficult at all to see how generational curses continue to plague our world. Racism, genocides, wars – these are all the results of historical happenings that continue to maintain a strangle-hold in today's world.

Learned behaviors, positive or negative, are perfectly capable of crossing generations, creating a new set of ripples with each crossing. You and I are powerless to change what has happened in the past, but we are certainly capable of impacting what *happens.* We have the power to make our own splashes and to create our own network of ripples, but this is not passive work. Making a change requires us *to do something.* Wishing and hoping are great past-times, but they don't achieve much. Each day, look for the chance to start your own ripple effect, and when the chance presents itself – take it! Keep, at the forefront of your mind, that your TODAY has the power to change someone's TOMORROW.

"Don't withhold good from someone who deserves it, when it is in your power to do so."

– Proverbs 3:27

CHAPTER 3

A BOTTLE OF WINE

Ding Dong!

The ringing of the doorbell caught us off-guard a little bit. We had just moved into the neighbourhood and knew absolutely no one in the quiet area that we were settling into. We paused from unboxing the dinnerware in the kitchen, exchanged quick quizzical glances, and then I headed to the door with an almost imperceptible shrug. Had it been in the nighttime, I would have probably grabbed something that had weapon-potential (just in case we were about to be greeted by one of those rare criminals with good manners) but since it was just before dusk, I was able to approach the door with sufficient confidence. Through the glass inserts I could tell that there was definitely a figure standing there – this wasn't a prank from the neighbourhood kids.

As I slowly opened the door (trying my best to minimize the squeaking of the unoiled hinges) I was greeted by the friendly disposition of a gentleman holding a bottle of blueberry wine in his hand. We weren't friends at the time, but he was not a stranger.

I had met Andrew a couple days earlier when we brought home the RV from the campground where we lived while we house-shopped. That particular day was the second time that I was ever towing the 32-foot 7,000lb behemoth of a trailer, and it was to be the first time that I was going to try my hand at precision parking the thing. The last time I tried this, I was out on an almost-empty campground with no immediate neighbours on either side. Even then, I still had to delegate parking duty to the host at the campground who made light work of what was threatening to undo my bowels. Now there was no camp host to call on, and the parking pad that was immediately next to our recently-acquired home was no more than 10 feet wide. There was sufficient reason for me to be sweating bullets on a chilly Fall afternoon.

I pulled up to the house and stopped on the side of the street. When my wife and kids arrived shortly after in her car, they met me standing on the driveway, deeply engaging my mental faculties as I calculated all the precise angles that I would need to execute in order to make this thing work. I stood there in silence, brow furrowed. She tried to ask me a question, but a quick rising of my open palm communicated that I was not in the mood to be bothered just then - this was serious business! I finished my recon exercise, jumped back in the truck, and selected the 'reverse' gear. About 7 seconds later the truck was back in 'park' and I was back in the driveway….'reconning' again. This time, I accommodated some conversation as it helped to drown out the intense battle that was raging in my head. My pride was screaming that I could do that which needed to be done, but every other fact of my being knew, quite matter-of-factly, that I was in way over my head.

It was then that I noticed an RV of similar dimensions parked quite neatly in the driveway of the house that was just across from ours, and a guy (who looked about my age) messing around with his truck in said driveway. I looked at my wife and thought about the admiration that she would have for me if I were to successfully park our trailer. I also thought of what the next few years of my life could look like if I were to inadvertently smash said trailer into the side of HER house. Before I finished imagining how the latter could unfold, my feet had already started walking me over to that neighbour's house to ask for help.

Andrew and his wife Irene had a beautiful family, complete with two sons, a daughter, and a dog. Their kids' ages lined up really nicely with ours, which made all the difference for a few birthday parties later on. I never quite found out what Irene did for a living, but Andrew worked at the local brewery. He was a local boy who had lived in Northern BC all his life and was therefore quite comfortable with the things that country living tends to expose you to – like towing and parking a trailer. I introduced myself as we exchanged pleasantries and handshakes. I stressed the handshakes just now because this was all happening in the height of the COVID-19 pandemic where human beings were treating each other like they were lepers. But not this guy, his hand came to me first and that told me all I would ever need to know about him. I explained the debacle in which I found myself and expressed my unfamiliarity with what was needed of me. He didn't smirk. He didn't scoff at me or take a jab at my ego (like most would). He dropped what he was doing and headed over to my truck.

Within two minutes there was a 32foot trailer parked next to our house. A marine helicopter pilot could not have dropped that trailer in that spot with any greater finesse than what I just witnessed. Once completed, he exited the truck and spent the next 5 to 10 minutes explaining to me the things to consider when reversing with a trailer. I smiled, nodded, and aahhed, but it all meant nothing to me. He welcomed us to the neighbourhood, and we parted ways pleasantly, never to cross paths again until about a week later when he showed up on our porch with a welcome gift. He had come to formally introduce himself and let us know that he would love for our families to be friends, especially as a social exercise for our kids.

The great neighbourly relationship lasted for the entire time that we lived in that community. The kids took turns visiting each house, Andrew and I have had the odd ping pong or badminton match - we got along quite well.

What he didn't know was that we kept that bottle of blueberry wine tucked in the back our fridge for all those years, unopened (not that I think he'd care). It just sat there, perpetually chilling and aging.

We have run through a few different ways to deal with that rogue bottle of wine in the fridge, which is only a problem because our home is an alcohol-free zone and neither of the adults are any kind of drinkers. The most obvious path of action that came to mind was to pop the cork and pour the content down the drain. But we nixed that idea because it just felt ungrateful and wasteful. We could also look up some recipes that call for blueberry wine and put our chef hats on, but that would put our tastebuds too far out of their predictable comfort zone. We could have also regifted the bottle, but why encourage the use of something that we do not subscribe to? Perhaps the best thing that we could have done, we thought, was to politely deny the gift when it was presented. Its just that Andrew had looked so genuine when he extended his hands that day, I just couldn't say no.

After a while, everyone stopped enquiring about that which was taking up valuable real estate inside the fridge and just came to accept it as a permanent fixture. But for me, it had a different meaning.

I have never shared it until now – it sounds silly enough inside my head – but that bottle of blueberry wine is a persistent reminder for me that there is hope for the goodness in humanity. It came to our doorstep from a stranger in a time when everyone was required by law to stay away from each other. Otherwise expressed, a stranger risked the social comforts of his family to make sure that newcomers to the area felt welcomed. That was big for me!

There are way too many well-founded reasons to be skeptical of humanity's future, and you don't have to go far to come across such reasons. There was a time when households would gather around their TV sets or radio at designated times to be brought up to speed on what is happening in the world. Shootings, robberies, rape cases, kidnappings, wars, bombing – those were once primetime TV content that had its faithful audience. I remember growing up and knowing that all rights to the TV were relinquished once 7pm rolled around. If I was dying, I would need to do so quietly because mommy and daddy were watching the news. The same would be true for the 8am news blast on the radio. You were allowed to speak before or after the news. Any attempt to speak during those 15mins was likely to be met with sharp, decisive (and often painful) force. Those days, it was easy to bury your head in the sand. Avoid the primetime reports and spend your money on snacks instead of reading the newspapers – you'd be fine. Those days are over!

With the advent of 24hr newsrooms, the internet, smartphones, and social media feeds, hopscotching your way through the minefield of media negativity is a task that will be met with failure more often than not. The-powers-that-be have even leveraged connectivity, using text message blasts to share news of kidnappings and shootings (which is actually a good initiative, but you get the point). There are daily happenings in the world that really begs the question of how much longer before we implode as global community.

There are days when the realities of life really weigh heavily on my shoulders, some are worse than others. But while so many who are similarly affected will go to their local corner bar and drown their sorrows with a few shots of something strong, I go home, open the door of my refrigerator and smile.

As long as there are people around, there will always be good people around. We should always be wise and careful in all our interactions. But there is reason to have faith in your neighbour, in your bus driver, in your mailman, and in your child's teacher. They may disappoint you, that's true. But what if they don't?

"Do to others as you would have them do to you." – Luke 6:31

CHAPTER 4

VIVA LAS VEGAS!

VEGAS BABYYYY!!!!

That's what everyone is supposed to yell when they are heading to that hedonistic oasis in the middle of the Nevada desert. History buffs seem to have a hard time agreeing on when exactly the city of Las Vegas got its name, but they all agree that it was a Spanish trader – Rafael Rivera – who gets the credit for labeling that patch of land. Over the years, however, 'The Meadows' (yes, that's the English translation for Las Vegas) has gradually transformed itself from a rest spot along the trade route between California and New Mexico, and is now identified as the party capital of North America.

Aptly referred to as 'Sin City', Las Vegas is the place where anything goes and where everything is acceptable….in theory. I intentionally added those two words just now because of the presence of a police force within the city, indicating that boundaries do exist in this other 'city that never sleeps'. But be that as it may, Las Vegas is well known for its overly forgiving nature and its ability to keep your darkest secrets ever so close to its drunken bosom. What happens in Vegas, stays in Vegas – until you sober up and check your credit card statement, forgetting to hide it from your suspicious spouse.

Well, I knew all of this, yet here I was all packed and ready to go, yelling for everyone to hurry and get their coats on so we could get on the road. I was going to Vegas, the city that seems to have all the action, and I wasn't going to miss that flight. What made this trip even more exciting was that I was going BY MYSELF!

Now I know what you're thinking, and I'll just stop you right there. This was not to be a stress-busting, liquor-infused, wallet-straining, hang-over-producing escapade dotted with questionable and infidelitous acts. I was on official business for my employer, tasked with bolstering the administrative depth of my department by attending a professional conference. My intentions were pure and undefiled, but I was still as excited as a puppy who saw his master headed to the treat jar. I couldn't wait to get on that plane.

Truthfully though, a part of me felt bad for leaving my wife and family all by themselves in the dead of winter. This was the middle of the final semester for my wife's second master's degree, and she was going to be dealing with all that comes with that, plus the feeding of four mouths (five if she decides to eat at any point), the shoveling of snow that was sure to come, and the cold temperatures that seldom rose above -20 degrees Celsius at that time of year. I did my best to secure what I could before I left. The cupboards and the fridge were stocked, the car's gas tank was full, tires and fluids were checked, and I made sure she knew where the emergency credit card was. She is a trooper through and through who had proven repeatedly that I really have no need to ever worry about her, but I still do.

On the one hand, I genuinely felt badly, unfair even, to be leaving her to hold down the fort by herself. But on the other hand, the thought of being in a place where I could walk outside without a jacket, scarf and gloves in February excited me more than a little bit.

We made it to the airport in time and after 2 uneventful flights spanning just over 8 hours, I stepped outside of the Harry Reid International Airport and breathed American air for the first time in my life. I had been to the USA twice before that day, but I was always connecting to other flights headed for other countries. This was the first time that I was to be walking American streets. I quickly realized that black, tar-and-gravel streets are pretty much the same regardless of where you went. There was no magic in the air, nor was there elevated ambience of the surroundings. My first deep breath was cut short by some guy who exhaled a lung-full of cigarette smoke in my direction. This was followed by the cab ride from hell that reminded me of my days growing up in the islands, where every bus or cab ride had the potential to be your last. I do remember being very impressed that my cab driver from the airport was able to hold a conversation while putting his car through its paces – he showed considerable skill in that regard. But other than that, my initial impressions of the place were not ones of awe. It was all just so-so.

But then morning came.

Maybe it was because I had a chance to get some much-needed sleep, or because my exchange with the very rude and dismissive desk clerk at my hotel was now reduced to a memory. But looking out the window of my room on the 33rd floor and watching the sun come up over the mountains on the horizon brought a solid smile to my face. It was a thing of absolute beauty, but one that I did not have all morning to enjoy. I had arrived the night before the conference was to start and the hotel where it was being held was a 12-minute walk away (according to google). I did what I do and got ready in record time, made a call back to Canada to get my morning dose of awesomeness from my home crew, and headed out on my virgin trek across Nevadan streets.

When I stepped outside of the hotel, I was awestruck! The streets were busy, the air was alive and bustling, and there was music booming from ghost speakers installed along the streets. Cars honked, engines revved, limousines cruised authoritatively along – everything that I beheld made a statement.

I identified the hotel that I needed to get to, but recognized that in order to get there, I would need to walk down the street, cross the overhead bridge, then walk back up the street to where I needed to be. That seemed dumb, but I had no time to argue with myself as I was late for breakfast. I hustled down the street and chuckled when I got the overhead bridge – there were escalators going up to and coming down from the overhead bridge.

Yes, you are right. Canada is not a backward country that is left in the past, we have escalators too. What I hadn't seen up to that point though was an escalator on the side of the road for the general public to use. My experiences with these moving stairs have always been indoors, in places of business. I never expected to see such machinations incorporated into a city's design. The civil engineers who came up with this earned their dollars in my opinion, especially since I was now going to be able to get the other side of the street much quicker than anticipated while saving myself some energy.

I made good use of those escalators and got to the buffet hall with only a few minutes to spare. I'm sure that my table manners that morning was a re-enactment of that restaurant scene in the 1995 movie 'Major Payne' (if you haven't seen that movie, you need to!), but I chose to not care in the moment as I had to finish my plate and get to the first session on time. I got there just in time, still chewing that last mouthful of eggs, and it was a great first session that paved the way for a rather enjoyable four-day event. My professional days gave way to evenings of roaming the streets, taking in the sights, and taking pictures like the tourist that I was. I made sure to order my steps wisely though. I was fully committed to being able to honestly recap every detail of my trip to my wife if I ever needed to – a mission that was only largely successful as I don't think she really needs to know exactly what my diet was like for that week.

I'll just continue to question the accuracy of our bathroom scale whenever we touch on that topic.

The escalator has come a far way since being unveiled in the late 1800s. Unlike most creations that tend to become more exquisite with time, the escalator has become less novel over the years. What was once a symbol of exclusivity is now very much expected and essentially common place. Whether it be for the sake of increased accessibility, or simply to provide another option for people as they move about, the escalator is now a staple in modern architecture and engineering. Regardless of how much respect is ascribed to the institution that boasts the moving stairs, its basic function of the escalator hasn't changed. It exists for the sole purpose of moving someone from point A to point B with reduced physical effort.

That part about 'reduced effort' is where the fitness buffs tend to get all in a tizzy though, and rightly so. Escalators, much like elevators, are formidable defenses against the exertion of climbing endless staircases. These assistive machines will get you to that important meeting looking a lot less disheveled and save your colleagues from having to listen to you wheeze your way back to a steady state. They are meant to improve the quality of life, though it may be correctly argued that the associated avoidance of physical activity is one of the many things that is wrong with today's society. I won't go down that rabbit hole. What I will do instead is to challenge the idea that 'the hard way is always the best way'. That is not true.

While I vehemently oppose any suggestion that a life of ease is the ideal that is to be pursued, I do believe that there is wisdom in allowing oneself to take advantage of opportunities when they come along. The fact that something comes easy is not enough to discredit its usefulness or to label it as dangerous. Like any other situation, critical thinking and careful analysis is to be applied to determine whether the step to be taken is indeed the right step. If, after the options have been weighed, it is decided that what is presented is indeed an opportunity and not a trap, the next step is to continue to take steps heading in the desired direction.

It is also wise to guard against the fear of moving ahead rapidly. There is nothing wrong with growing and getting ahead quickly if the condition is right to do so. I am not one to be easily annoyed, but seeing healthy, able-bodied people standing still on an escalator really grinds my gears. Yes – I am fully aware that this is 'the purpose' of an escalator, but is it not obvious that a quicker ascension would be possible if they were to continue to climb the steps as the steps go up? Even at the slowest climbing pace, it is a GUARANTEE that they will reach the top faster than they would have if they were standing still. This is a trap that many persons fall for in their journey through life, both personally and professionally. They work hard, finish school, get that degree (or those degrees), land a good job, then sit back and wait on the ladder that they are on to take them to the top.

For some, that might work. Their work ethic, favor with the boss, and connections with the right people will see them moving through life and climbing the ranks with relative ease – like they were on an escalator. But so much more could have been theirs within a much shorter period of time if the drive that was there in the early days was allowed to continue having a place in their journey. Standing still on the escalator will still get a person from point A to point B, but those that keep their feet churning while on these moving staircases will get there faster than if they had just planted their feet.

The need to push when times are hard is obvious – how else should one expect to make it through whatever the challenge is in the moment? But pushing when times are easy is often of greater benefit because:

- It gives a head start on the tough times (that are sure to come)
- It helps create breathing room for those times when you need to take a break
- You get farther faster, and with less effort

The successful journey does not consist of sporadic surges of great effort. To the contrary, continuous and consistent effort towards identified goals creates a life of success.

"Commit to The Lord whatever you do, and He will establish your plans." – Proverbs 16:3

CHAPTER 5

Fender Benders

She was dirty and she idled a bit rough. The seats had some rips and the knobs for the air conditioning system were only decorative, but she was mine!

Like most young boys, I had dreamed and waited for this day with bated breath – the day that I would have my very own car. That day came a little late for me (at age 21), but that's just how long it took to save up and, perhaps, my ability to borrow my dad's minivan or my older brother's chick-mobile from time to time fostered a bit of complacency.

The wait was over though. Here I stood, handing over the worn stack of bills that would make my ownership of this 1989 Suzuki Cultus GTi official. I had followed my watchful brother's advice and had kept up a stoic appearance during negotiations, being careful not to show too much interest, even though I was ready to sell my mother's kidney for that car. You see, not only was this machine going to solidify my status as an independent adult. It was also going to be the third such car in my circle of friends! A motor club was being born and it felt good to be a part of it. I left the seller's home that Sunday evening with only the registration and the car keys as I would need to go the government office in the morning to complete the transfer and get registration plates.

The usual antics of our resident mosquitoes were no bother to me that night since my eyes simply refused to close. The morning was taking too long to arrive and I was dead set on being up with the first ray of the rising sun. I was at the government office before the doors opened for the usual Monday morning rush. As soon as the last lock was undone on those doors, I moved with Spiderman-like stealth, agility, and accuracy to get to the front of the line and to be among the first 5 to be seen. By mid-morning I had reconnected with my brother Colin and we were headed down the boulevard to go and collect MY car.

Greetings and pleasantries exchanged; license plates attached; engine started….and away we went!

I was certain that everyone could hear me grinning from a mile away. As I headed home, I couldn't help but feel like we were meant for each other. I was changing gears with precision, clutching at precisely the right time, and navigating the post-rush-hour traffic like a Schumacher knock-off. So you can imagine how far and hard my heart sank when the car suddenly died about 5 mins from home. Without warning, at a busy intersection, the engine had just died and decided that restarting was not an option. Instead of taking her home, giving her a good cleaning and showing her to my dad when he got home from work (like I had planned), my little blue trophy went straight to a mechanic's shop.

As much as it hurt in the moment, I was still excited (don't ask me how that works). I mean, this was all by design…..sort of.

I was at that age where everyone I knew was buying cars. A good bunch of those purchasers chose to take out a car loan and buy a used vehicle from one auto establishment or another. I didn't want to do that. My philosophy was that I needed to know enough about maintaining and/or fixing a car before treating myself to a 'new vehicle'. I was going to do all in my power to avoid being *that guy* who had to call his friend each time the car coughed. When Little Blue broke down that morning, I received confirmation that this car had a lot to teach me. As a child of the 80's who did not escape the allure of the Transformers movies, you could call this my Bumblebee moment. I would continue to depend on public transport for the next 6 days while my car was being repaired and tuned. I would soon get the call that all was done and that I was free to pick up at my convenience. I was at the shop within an hour after ending that call, and soon drove off as a proud car-owner - again.

Well, as is the case for almost everyone who has ever owned a car, the relationship between Little Blue and myself was not to last forever. The 6 months that we shared left me with nothing but good memories. From street races to drag races, early morning road trips to late night escapades, numerous trips to the gas pump and several trips to the shop - Blue and I went through it all and we always had each other's back. Had it not been for the fateful Saturday morning crash, our time together would have likely continued for a few more months. I mean, I knew that our time would eventually end since my learning plan demanded that I change vehicles over time. But, truth be told, I would have much preferred to do so voluntarily than to have the decision made for me. Connecting with the guard rail of the highway while going 100km/hr was not part of the plan. And if it wasn't for the bus that had come into my lane and forced me to decelerate from the 180km/hr that I was doing just seconds before, the story of my life could have ended that morning.

I lost Little Blue and would go on to own 17 more cars over the next 19 years, telling myself that this was all a part of my work up to owning a brand-new vehicle. There was an element of truth to this, yes, but I also tended to get bored with the vehicles I owned and would change them every six months (on average). However, the day finally came when I felt I was ready to settle down. My 40th birthday was coming up and, since life supposedly begins at 40, it was time for me to take the bull by the horns, walk onto into a dealership and drive out in something that had the never-before-experienced and heretofore elusive 'new car smell'!

I traveled 8 hours away from home to get to **'Stryker'!** Stryker was a Bright White Ram 1500 Big Horn, magnificent in her simplicity and effortlessly seductive. The dealership had robbed me of the chance to peel the plastic from her seat, but I got to remove the protective film from the touchscreen radio. The rush of emotion was almost like I was getting married all over again. My first order of business, after pronouncing a blessing over her, was to attend a virtual meeting from the cockpit (curse the COVID-19 'work from anywhere' virus). After that, the next few days were all about discovering how to handle this specimen of cutting-edge engineering. The 15 months that followed would see me doing minor modifications to make her mine as I was dead-set on having this vehicle long enough to pass it down to one of my youngsters.

I gave my eldest her first driving lesson in that truck, the one that she had come to love almost as much as she loved me. Stryker was a family hit! And that is why it hurt so badly when I broadsided that careless driver on my way to work on what had previously been just another Tuesday.

It was on a wet November morning, having just done the school drop-offs and heading into the office, that I was given the reminder of how uncertain life can be. I wasn't a speedster anymore (wife and kids tend to tame the daredevil in you) so I was doing a very responsible speed heading down the road when my peripheral vision picked up the old brown truck moving perpendicularly towards the highway. The road was busy enough, as we were in the height of rush hour, so he was obviously going to stop at the stop sign and wait his turn. That was the expectation, but….nope!

'Grandpa' proceeded out into the roadway, attempting to cross two lanes to get to the other side, only managing to cross one. There was nowhere for me to go and no time or space for me to stop. The T-Bone was inevitable. The side of his built-like-a-tank old truck was dented, but the front my self-gift was a mangled heap of metal and broken plastic. I was in shock! If I was one who drank enough water and was well-hydrated I would have cried. I wasn't angry at him, even though he had decided to get behind the wheel of a vehicle without a valid driver's license and tempt the hand of fate. I was just sad and heartbroken.

The morning that started like any other ended with me standing out in the cold drizzle, watching my dream being carted away on a flatbed tow truck.

I never spoke to the other driver at all, the police wouldn't let me. Perhaps they thought I would have attacked him.

Perhaps they were right.

The earliest mathematical sessions that you are likely to recall, after learning to count sequentially, would have centered around arithmetical operation. We learn to add and subtract. We learn the rules and steps that govern such operations, principles that are written in stone and are integral to much of your educational future. We learn that 2 + 2 must add up to 4, and that the sum of 5 and 5 is always 10. Well, guess what? In life, that linearity isn't always true. The harsh truth is that the results we receive are not always guaranteed by the steps taken along the way.

Life would be much easier to deal with, to accept, if we could rest assured that we will always receive the just reward for the work we put in. Getting up, going into the office and working hard everyday would be much more fulfilling if you didn't keep getting passed over for that promotion. It would be easier to face each day if we knew, without the shadow of a doubt, that doing things the right way would protect us from untoward occurrences.

But it just doesn't work like that. It never has, and it never will. Bad things happen to good people and disasters arise without provocation. Bible-believers understand what is going on behind the curtains, but on the world stage, it is a difficult and heart-wrenching reality. Loving your children does not guarantee that they will love you back. Healthy living does not guarantee a long life. Loyalty to friends is not always reciprocated. Driving safely will not always protect you from a collision.

It….just….doesn't….work that way, no matter how much we wish it would.

The trick is to understand that setbacks are not final and knock-downs do not have to be knock-outs. Taking the time to grieve an injustice is natural, and recommended, but that grieving period should ALWAYS be temporary. Recognizing that you are only able to control what goes on within you is the first step towards being able to handle whatever life throws at you. Move past the unsolicited events that seem to challenge the ideals of your life and remain focused on where you hope to be. The vicissitudes of life will gradually lose power.

"Look straight ahead and fix your eyes on what lies before you. Mark out a straight path for your feet; stay on the safe path. Don't get sidetracked…." – Proverbs 4:25 - 27

CHAPTER 6

THE LAWNMOWER AND ME

Grandkids are supernaturally empowering!

So very often I have been able to observe the merciless dismantling of the most stoic and rigid personalities by the smiles and giggles of a grandchild. I'm not a grandpa as yet, and I keep telling my eldest girl that I am in no hurry to wear that title – though that sentiment is more of a caution to her than it is my avoidance of growing old. Regardless of my relative youthfulness, I am now old enough to have a few grandparents in my circle of friends and in every instance that I am able to observe these friends of mine interacting with their progeny, there presents a light in their eye and a pep in their step that would otherwise lie dormant. It is as if the little ones impart a buoyancy that helps to create a care-free environment, which I have seen to produce both good and bad outcomes.

Grandbabies will inspire grandma to don her apron and bake up a storm, just by saying "may I have a cookie?". Grandsons are often recipients of lessons in fishing and carpentry that their parent was never privy to. This is not to say that Grandma and Grandpa were bad parents. To the contrary, I have come to realize that for these mature folk, it is often the case that their focus on creating a good life for their children in yesteryears required them missing certain opportunities that retirement now allows them to enjoy with their grandkids. It is a sad truth, but it is the truth. A few years ago, I had the chance to benefit greatly from such a scenario, in a very convoluted and indirect way.

My family had just immigrated to Canada and we were settling into the city of London, a quasi rural city in Southwestern Ontario. We had been befriended by a wonderful woman by the name of Teresa (you will see that name again in this book) and she was a true gem of a human. My wife – the immutable introvert – hit it off with Teresa as if they knew each other from a previous life. Never mind the 30year age gap and the fact that they were from different sides of the world, they were like sisters from the get-go. I kept my distance though. I had to ensure that at least one of us remained impartial so that we could objectively evaluate the intentions of 'this strange woman'. Time would eventually show me just how silly I was, but what can I say? I take my job as *protector of my family* very seriously!

It was while I was busy keeping my distance that I got the opportunity to receive another valuable educational moment. Teresa's husband, Valdermar, is a man's man like no other. If ever there was one man who could truthfully say that "he pulled himself up his own bootstraps", it was Valdemar. A navy man turned construction genius with a passion for farming, he was generally a man of very few words. If, however, you were to get him talking about his life experiences, you would do well to pull up a chair and cancel all of your appointments for the rest of the day. He could talk for hours about his struggles as a child, his years in the navy, his Christian journey, his sibling relationships, his wife and children…..he would go on and on! But he was so good at telling his story that on those rare occasions when he would actually open up, the audience could effortlessly listen for hours and never get bored. Some people imprison others with their conversations – pushing the listeners to look for any opportunity to end the conversation and run. Valdemar, on the other hand, would arrest your attention to the point where you end up completely ignoring the food that Teresa would be piling onto the table without pause.

Initially, I was only acquainted with Valdemar because he was Teresa's husband. We did the occasional "hi and bye" when we crossed paths, but that would be the extent of it – until my wife learned of an accident that had left him bruised and battered. Apparently, a visit from those empowering grandkids of his had somehow led to Valdemar rigging up a tree swing in his backyard. He then made the (somewhat silly) decision to test his creation, simultaneously giving the kids a demonstration of its use. This act, noble as it was, was rewarded with a pretty nasty fall that landed him in the emergency department of the local hospital and left him with a few cracked ribs. This would have been tough for anyone at any age. But this vibrant, active golden ager was not at all amused by what this meant for him. He had to slow down for a while and avoid any heavy-duty activities. For Valdemar, you may as well had put him in prison. As simple a task as mowing the lawn would mean excruciating pain, and this was what set the stage for our relationship to take a turn for the better.

When my wife learned of his injury and ensuing challenges, she – without hesitation (or appropriate consultation) – offered up her able-bodied husband to go and help with the yard work. To this day I don't know what she was thinking! At the time that all this was unfolding, my horticultural expertise was limited to picking fruits from trees and raking leaves. What was I going to do on Valdemar's well-manicured property in the middle of summer? It would have made more sense if we were talking about the Fall when the trees were shedding their leaves – a rake is not that hard to figure out. But gardening?! I was simply being set up for failure! Nevertheless, I'm sure you can surmise that I didn't have much say in the matter. I was unceremoniously seconded to Teresa and Valdemar's residence and was politely made to understand that it was not a negotiation.

On the agreed Friday afternoon, I left work, went home, changed into some old clothes, and then drove out to perform my duties. When I got there, all of my fears were realized. I looked at the neatly arranged flower beds, the sharp boundaries of the backyard lawn, the various flower bushes that would need some hedging, and I began to sweat bullets. To some, none of this would seem like a big deal – its all just plants. But a cursory glance at the surroundings made it abundantly clear that this man took his landscaping seriously and I was afraid of making a complete fool of myself. I was so relieved when he said that he only needed help with cutting the grass. I could see that it was a little over-grown (not too badly in my opinion) but if that's what he wanted done then that's what I would do. He then ducked into his shed and pulled out something that sent shivers up my trembling spine……a lawn mower!

We never had a green grassy lawn space in our home where we grew up. We had a huge East Indian Mango tree in the front yard and three other fruit trees in the back. Though my father tried on several occasions to get a lawn going, the competing trees with their wide branches and thick foliage never gave the grass a chance. What we did get was thick brambly brush and those were kept in check by my dad's trusty machete.

I would often watch him swing that tool with such ease, poise and precision, getting nice level cuts all across the yard. That responsibility was eventually passed on to my older brother and he was equally masterful, though his technique was a little different than that of our dad since he is left-handed. It wasn't long until I felt the need to follow in their footsteps, but I never had the coordination. My swings always landed in the dirt, sending pebbles flying in every direction. My persistent spirit would see me wearing goggles to keep the dirt from my eyes because believe me, it was nothing short of a sandstorm when I went out there. I tried my best to develop 'that skill', but I never did quite get the hang of it. When my brother left home and my dad's back started to act up, we started paying someone to come and do the cutting. I had to accept defeat.

In all of this, I had never had the good fortune or the opportunity to touch a lawn mower. We never owned one, so I had no experience with one.

With that snippet of my childhood replaying in my mind, I stood there staring at the scary machine that Valdemar had just placed in front of me. I had a choice to make here: I could either confess that I don't know how to use a simple machine that many 12-year-olds use to earn summer money, or I could grab the handle bar and fake it.

I decided that I was not going to fold. I confidently smiled and walked up to the grass cutting contraption. I fiddled with it, shook it around, rocked it back to look underneath, check the wheels to make sure they were well-attached – I gave it a good inspection because I wanted to make sure it was fit for the job. That was the impression I was trying to give, at least. In actuality, I was stalling and acting like I knew what I was doing, while I tried to think of a way to get out of this no-win situation. If only my phone would ring and allow me to fake an emergency that would require my urgent departure…..but the cursed thing remained silent!

My heart fluttered with joy when I heard Valdemar say, " this can be finicky to start, so let me get it going.".

Crisis averted!

I stood back and respectfully motioned for him to give it a go. It took him a couple of pulls but soon, the engine was roaring away. He motioned me back over, I took the handlebar from him, and I started to hack away at the grass.

You might have driven past those houses with the big front lawns and seen those really neat, symmetrically cut lines in the grass after a fresh cut. Those straight, parallel lines are testament to a true master gardener, and it was those lines that I was aiming for. I knew what I wanted to do, I had the lines in my head, I just couldn't get them in the grass. As I looked over the areas that I covered and noticed that I was doing a less than stellar job, I started to stress-sweat like crazy; and catching a glimpse of Valdemar's furrowed brow only made it worse.

Just as embarrassment was starting to sink all the way in, I saw him motioning for me to stop. I did. He came over to me and asked directly, "have you ever done this before?"

The jig was up! It would make no sense for me to lie now as the proof of my inexperience was all across the backyard. A shy, embarrassed smile crept across my face as I fessed up to my pretense. If that lawnmower had gone rogue and taken a couple toes off my foot right then and there, it would not have hurt as much as my pride was hurt in that moment. I was embarrassed beyond belief! Ashamed of my utter uselessness to this real-life commando no less.

I fully expected some witty comment or humbling jab to come my way. Instead, I felt a callous hand brush mine as Valdemar gently rescued the lawnmower from my grip and said five words, "let me show you how". He was in obvious pain as we went across the lawn a couple of times, me soaking up every little tip or trick he was offering. I eventually finished up the yard, and it wasn't half bad by the time I was done. Even Valdemar was surprised at how good it turned out, telling me he was just as nervous about my ability as I was in the first place.

Michael Manley was the fourth Prime Minister of the Island of Jamaica. After taking office in 1972, one of his legacy projects was the implementation of the Jamaican Movement for the Advancement of Literacy (JAMAL). JAMAL was to support adults in their basic literacy journey, creating a solid platform for life-long learning. Though this initiative was quite noble, there was a mindset among the Jamaican people that would inhibit the intended impact. The Jamaica back then was a lot more blue-collar than the Jamaica of today and it was not uncommon for adults to have very low literacy levels, especially in rural communities. The harsh realities of the struggling country would frequently force children to trade schooling for working on family farms or getting odd jobs to ease the burden on their parents. For adults who would have gone through that rite of passage, so to speak, a JAMAL-affiliated learning center represented their second chance – their beacon of hope.

However, a stigma was quickly attached to those places of learning with the more affluent labeling JAMAL attendees as stupid and 'dunce' (a local derogatory term used to describe an illiterate). It was no wonder then that attendance at these centers would gradually wane as the years went by as no one wanted to be thought of as less-than. That kind of thinking, not unique to Jamaica, eventually resulted in much negativity being ascribed to Life-Long-Learning. It became taboo to go back to school in adult years unless you were seeking an advanced or graduate credential. In other words, learning as an adult was only acceptable if you were learning adult things. If you missed it as a child, it is better for you to die without it than to go back and try to fill that gap. Any attempt to right the wrong of a missed opportunity in younger years was a display of weakness and would be akin to painting a target on your own back.

Why it took so long for the related lightbulb to go off for me? I don't know. But Valdemars's action on that hot Friday afternoon opened up my eyes like never before. There is no shame in admitting that "I don't know." No two people on earth would have walked identical paths in their lives, and that disparity guarantees a difference in experience, exposure and learning opportunities. It is therefore unfair to assume the knowledge base of those we interact with, and even worse to tie their value to what they are supposed to know when we have had no hand in teaching them anything. One of the purposes of community is to support and complete each other. If everyone knew everything then no one would need anyone, and like it or not, we all need somebody.

Our action toward those that demonstrate a gap in their knowledge base tells a lot about who we truly are. Valdemar could have laughed me to scorn that day. He could have scoffed at my lack of exposure, questioned my preparation to have a home and family of my own, and chased me off his lawn in true grandpa fashion. But he didn't. On that day, he chose to share some of what he has with someone who lacked. And in doing so, he bandaged up a young man's wounded pride, laid the foundation for the development of a new skill that has brought many compliments to the young man's cars. He gave the young man something else that he can pass on to his children, and he did all that by saying 5 words and sharing 2 minutes of his afternoon.

We are all learners, and we are all teachers. Sometimes we are one or the other, and sometimes we are both simultaneously. You can only give what you have, you are the only one who has what you have, and there is bound to be someone who needs what you have. Let Valdemar's five words be your motto and you will change the world one lesson at a time.

"So encourage each other and build each other up…." 1 Thessalonians 5:11

CHAPTER 7

FALLING LEAVES

I stood in the que at the grocery store. What was supposed to be a quick Sunday morning errand was dragging along at a snail's pace. The store was uncharacteristically busy, which meant I had to wait a lot longer to voluntarily empty my pockets in exchange for over-priced examples of the shrink-flation phenomenon, but I stood somewhat patiently biding my time.

There was the elderly woman in front of me who was trying to figure out how to insert her credit card into the cashier's point-of-sale machine. I wanted to commend the cashier on her patience and generally pleasant demeanor, even though the innocent grandma was obviously testing her boundaries. But protocol demanded that I mind my own business and pretend to not be eavesdropping on the exchange happening 8 feet in front me. I focused my attention elsewhere, landing on the well-dressed young woman who decided that this cold, snowy day was the perfect time to try out her new high-heel boots. I moved my gaze again because I was sure things were going to take a turn for the worse in very short order.

Then along comes "the couple" – a middle aged man who was more-than-a-little pudgy around the middle, long gray beard, wearing a hoodie and baseball cap. He was walking behind a woman who looked to be of similar age, casually dressed in blue jeans and a loose-fitting top, but it was obvious that he was not enjoying the trip. He might have been dutifully carrying the grocery bin, but his unnecessarily tight grip on the handles betrayed the tense conversation that must have preceded their entry into the store. As they passed by my que, I noticed that his hoodie had something written on it:

"I don't Suck At Hunting,
Animals Suck At Standing in Front Of Me."

I chuckled because I could relate.

I am no hunter. I didn't grow up around hunters and none of my friends ever let on that they even had the inclination. I saw my dad butcher a goat once when I was 6 or 7 years old, and I remembered helping my neighbor process chickens from her backyard coop in my early teens. Other than that, I did my hunting in the freezers at the grocery stores. That's not to say I didn't try to revisit the ways of our ancestors from time to time. On any one of those rare Autumn mornings that I could carve out a few hours for myself, I would be up with the sun and off to find some logging roads, hoping that a game bird would be dumb enough to just stand in front of me.

There was also another reason that I would look forward to those mornings, and it might not make sense to too many (it didn't really make sense to me until I experienced it myself), but there is just something utterly therapeutic about silence in the outdoors. Yes, I will agree that my appreciation of solitude might be tied to the rarity of its occurrence, with my household being what it is, but I really look forward to those early morning wanderings. Just me, a gentle breeze, the crunching of gravel under my boots, and the falling leaves.

Yes! I said the falling leaves!

Again, you will not believe it until you've had the experience. But it is possible to hear the leaves as they fall from the limbs of those spruce or poplar trees, hitting neighbouring leaves and bounding from branch to branch until they settle on the forest floor with a soft rustle. Its almost orchestral – at least to my ears.

In all the music though, the reality is not lost on me that these trees – each one an integral part of the surrounding forest – are shedding their beauty as they prepare for the winter. Some say that this happens because the trees are beginning to store their nutrients in their branches and trunks for the winter. Other schools of thought are a lot more scientific, blaming hormonal changes in the trees (if you can believe it) for the loss of leaves. I am in no way inclined to attempt the debunking of any of those ideologies via this forum. All I know is that there would be trees that were full and lusciously green just a few weeks before that would transform into a dull, brown, almost bare form of their past selves. Birds would lose their nesting spaces and shaded spots would become scarce.

From the ground, I could certainly tell the difference and, I am sure, it was noticeable to the ravens that were flying above my head. There is a certain element of sadness to it all, but what can I say? Its just part of the process…I guess.

Leaves fall and they regrow. That's just the way nature is programmed. I know! – not all trees are subject to this cycle, but this cycle comes with the territory for most plant species, stopping only when a tree is dead or cut down. We know and accept that principle. But what if we were open to learning from that principle? In what other areas of life might it be applied? To describe something as 'deteriorating' is to suggest that it is undergoing a negative change. That *thing* is undergoing a transformation that will see it losing some of its inherent value. I have seen this process play out many times. Family members, colleagues or regular acquaintances suddenly, or gradually, begin to behave in ways that are uncharacteristic for them. For example, my colleagues may start to lose their drive or enthusiasm. Their work loses the usual pizzazz, their attitudes begin to sour, their smiles start to fade, and often, in those instances, I might begin to worry, withdraw, observe, and fortify my own walls against the expected spin-offs.

If these persons are your peers, the natural reaction is to protect your own interest. If they are on their way down, if they are going to be summoned to the boss' office, the natural response is to do all that is reasonable to ensure that they go down alone. You do all you can to ensure that you are not caught in the crossfire when things go sideways.

If these behaviours are being seen in subordinates, the boss will likely begin to contemplate the strength of his/her succession plan – analyzing who might be in the best position to take over the reins of 'the dead-weight'. When it is the boss that is starting to show signs indicative of a decline, everybody starts to dress sharper, get to work earlier, work harder, speak louder, trying to get the attention of the boss' boss as this might just be the break that they've been waiting for.

But what if we, instead, choose to see falling leaves as an opportunity to nurture a tree that is going through its own cycle? What if we choose to remember the luscious, vibrant, bountiful tree that used to be, believing that there remains a potential for regrowth?

A farmer does not take an axe to every tree that loses its leaves. As a matter of fact, I'll confess that one of the big battles that occurred in my marriage came because I (prematurely) took some shears to a plain, withered-down eye sore. An attempt at executing a perfect post-winter yard cleanup saw me unceremoniously desecrating my wife's favorite plant in the yard. I still can't recall the name of the tree, but I do remember justifying my actions by pointing out that there wasn't a single leaf on the branches, and that the brutally cold winter had obviously killed the tree. I was wrong, of course, but the fire in my wife's eyes and the thunder in her voice as she showed me the error of my ways will haunt me till the end of my days. That particular tree has earned permanent and irrevocable protection from my pruning shears and shall enjoy said protection until I am visited by the angel Gabriel with plain instructions to the contrary. I was firmly scolded (for days on end), and rightly so, for being too quick to act in a destructive manner, which is a demonstration of a mindset that is way too prevalent today.

Our society tends to give up on people much too quickly. The recognition that life is cyclical, and that there will be peaks and troughs in our personal, social, spiritual, and professional lives is becoming foreign. We hold each other to such high standards that people are becoming afraid to struggle, afraid to voice their challenges, afraid to be honest. To be "damaged" is now synonymous with being "useless" and nothing could be further from the truth. We won't all go through our *winters* at the same time, but cold and brutal seasons are guaranteed for everyone that is to walk this earth. Realizing and accepting that allows us to be more open to supporting each other when the chips are down.

It would be good for us to remember that the (almost) bare trees that surround us in the Fall are only shadows of their former selves, and that they are guaranteed to look completely different in due time if conditions that are suitable for regrowth come back around. Time and patience are often all that are needed. We sometimes need to bring ourselves to afford some time and patience to that colleague or neighbor who seems to be falling off their game. It is true, some may be struggling in ways that need stronger intervention, but others might just be going through something and need someone to believe in them while they restart; they may need someone to create the conditions that will help them through their process.

In either case, it is not usually wise to define someone by their worst day. Instead, try to see past the surface. Share a smile, give a compliment, leave an anonymous treat on a desk. Let that 'failing tree' in your midst know that you are looking forward to their Spring!

"Love never gives up on people. It never stops trusting, never loses hope, never quits." –

1 Corinthians 13:7

CHAPTER 8

LEGACY

At what point does a boy become a man?

When does a little girl officially cross the threshold from ribbons-and-curls to lipstick-and-heels?

There are more than a few different measuring sticks for this life-altering, pivotal moment, and I dare say that each criterion is subject to the preference or interpretation of the subject in question.

For example, the youngster who dreams of being behind the steering wheel of dad's old truck will want to claim adulthood the day before his sixteenth birthday. However, that same 'adult' will be happy to wear the title of 'juvenile' until way past their 18th birthday just to avoid getting a full-time job and paying their own bills.

Then there is the external standpoint to consider. Most countries will happily collect the taxes of anyone who is 18 years old or above and allow them to have their say at the election polls but will withhold the freedom to visit the local watering hole for a little while longer – sometimes until the third decade of life. There is also the loving wife who embraces her husband's *adult* ambitions as he climbs the corporate ladder but continues to dictate when or what he can or cannot eat. The term "adult" means different things to different people at different times – that is just the reality of it all.

One thing that can hardly be debated though is that at some time or another, we will all get to the place where we consider ourselves to be adults. We have endured the years of following orders, being burdened with endless homework and house chores. We have paid our dues and built up enough life experience (or so we think) to take on the world and forge our own path into the great unknown. We beat our own drums and march to our own beat – if only in our heads.

But is that all? Did we go through all that we did, and learn as much as we could, just so that we can claim to have arrived?

Some may say, "yes!" without hesitation.

But is there no greater purpose to one's journey than to give a few self-pats on the shoulder and gloat about their graduation from The School of Hard Knocks?

Don't get me wrong - I get it! I completely understand the innate tendency to celebrate triumphs over obstacles that have left countless others down for the count. As a matter of fact, I encourage it! I believe that there is need to recognize and acknowledge when things have actually gone right in our lives. This world presents us with more than enough reason and opportunity to be despondent, even to the point of being afraid to get out of bed on some days. So why should one not blow the celebratory trumpet on the (often) rare occasion where the 'stars align' in their favor? He should blow that trumpet for as loud and as long as he can! But he who have overcome must now allow himself to be a guiding light to those that are still finding their way. This point was reinforced to me in a most unlikely instance.

A group of men from my local church in London, Ontario had learned that one of our beloved older couples needed some work done on their house. This was a charming couple who had put their time in, worked hard in their younger days, and decided – in their sunset years – to adopt two twin girls who were under the age of 10. I mention this just to give a glimpse into the character of this couple – they both had hearts the size of Lake Superior!

When the call came for workers to assemble and help out this couple, the response was just what you would expect. As the sun came out on the agreed-upon Sunday morning, there was quite a respectable group of men gathered at the house, all ready to do their part in helping this well-loved couple. The group consisted of seasoned construction workers, others who were simply well-intentioned, men with carpentry background, able-bodied laborers, energetic teenage boys (present mostly for the camaraderie and the promise of a free lunch), and then there was me!

Let me point out here that the way I listed the breakdown of the group above is not coincidental. Up until that day that I am referring to, the extent of my construction experience was when I helped my father to build a small work-table for my mother, and by 'help', I mean 'hand him a nail when he asked for it'. I knew nothing about anything related to home or roof repair, I was uncomfortable with heights, I had no experience with a nail-gun…I could go on, but you get my drift. I had no reason showing up to help re-shingle a roof. But I was determined to lend a hand to a church brother and sister because that was the Christian thing to do.

I got up early that Sunday morning, picked up the still-spotless tool belt that had been gifted to me on the preceding Father's Day, grabbed my Dollar store hammer and set out to work. When I got to the worksite, I had my game face on like you would never believe. I climbed the ladder with so much confidence even though my heart had taken up residence in the back of my throat, and I joined the team in removing the old shingles. In fact, I did a pretty good job at that part. In no time we had the bare ply-boards of the roof exposed, cleaned and ready for the roof underlayment and ice shield. By the time that the glory of the mid-morning sun was upon us, my shirt was wet with sweat as I passed the shingles and the roofing nails to the men who actually knew what they were doing.

Lunch break came at around noon, and it was a welcome break. The work-bee team came down to a fantastic spread that had been put together by the lady of the house and her army of veteran home-makers who were there to make sure that no one passed out from hunger or exhaustion. From the home-made lasagna to oven-roasted chicken, the garden salad to watermelon slices, everyone present was able to eat their fill in preparation for an intense evening of more work. It was while we sat at the table, embroiled in light-hearted chatter, that this lesson on mentorship was driven home to me in a remarkable way.

Pastor Alex, a God-fearing man with a penchant for being heavenly-minded while being mindful of his place on earth, was the *foreman* of our impromptu construction team. He had done his time in construction in his life before pastoral ministry. but he was always on the lookout for the next building repair project to jump into. As we talked over lunch, the conversation somehow got around to the challenges that rambunctious teenagers can present in various circumstances. You see, there was one teen who had showed up for work that day that probably would not have been terribly missed if he had decided to just sleep in. I will respectfully refer to this boy as 'Larry'.

Now before I start to rag on Larry too much, I will state for the record that I watched him grow into quite a responsible leader in the years that followed. The mountain of trouble that he was, somehow became an example to the youngsters around him – a growth that lends credence to the point of this chapter.

On the Sunday morning in question, however, Larry – somewhere around 16 years of age at the time - had shown up just as loud and playful as he ever was. The entire morning saw us reminding him of the neighbors and the fact that many of them were probably still in bed. He would walk around the roof doing precious little - similar to what I was doing - but he did it in a much more annoying way. I for one was wanting to send him home, and I wasn't alone. Others felt the same way but since he had not driven there, he was only going to leave when his ride was ready to go and his ride was actually one of those who knew what they were doing. So we were bound to put up with him for the day.

For the morning, I had managed to keep my composure about the entire thing. But then lunchtime came, I began conversing with Pastor Alex, and before I knew what had happened my frustration had escaped my lips. I was partially embarrassed, since I was part of the church's youth leadership that was supposed to see only the good in our youth, but I also felt some amount of relief as I was able to say how I really felt. Pastor Alex responded in his characteristically blunt persona. He was able to scold you so skillfully that though his words were very direct and honest, you did not feel the full brunt of them until later in the evening as you drifted off to sleep. Very rarely was one able to lash out at Pastor Alex since he would often offend you in his absence.

This day though, his words hit me like a roofing hammer between the eyes. He was honest enough to acknowledge the challenge that was Larry, but rather than dismissing him the way I wanted to, he instead suggested that Larry be kept in our company as often and for as long as he wanted to. My point of contention was that Larry acted way too childishly for his age. Pastor Alex's response:

"How can you expect him to act like a man if men never take the time to teach him how to act?"

Just let that sink in for a minute............

It is often the expectation of adults that children will naturally move through the different stages of their development, from childhood to adulthood, with only the occasional guidance of a stern word or some form of strong discipline being necessary. Apparently, somewhere within the human psyche is a well-hidden guidance chip that will trigger the appropriate change in behavior, focus, ambition, mannerism, aptitude, and character as the child moves from year to year. Pastor Alex did not subscribe to that thinking and I have since seen the wisdom in his viewpoint.

The adults of today have the responsibility of mentoring the adults of tomorrow. Most of us will do our part to ensure that we impart good values and ethics to our own children. But how often do we think about the fact that our children share this world with others who are not members of our family? If every man's focus is only on those who belong to him, then he should be aware that he is not doing very well at protecting their future.

My daughter recently shared one of her many favorite YouTube videos with me. This one was about a pair of boxing prodigies – Daniel and Steven Grandy – who are set to shine in the world of boxing. While that particular video was meant to showcase the extraordinary command of the sport that these 10-year-old twin boys had, it was a statement made by their coach-father that got me. He shared that he not only trained his sons to box, he actually trained many other children in his community and his reason for doing so was simply this: "the more kids I can train, the less chance one of those kids could pick up a gun and shoot one of my kids….".

The effects of mentorship last longer and reach farther than is often perceivable. The last time I met Larry I was pleasantly surprised to see him volunteering in a leadership role at his local church. The boy who once cause grown men and women to run for cover was now front and center – teaching life skills to children in an organized community outreach program. Was that Pastor Alex's doing? No doubt he had a hand in it.

A legacy that will return incalculable dividends has been left in a young boy's heart because a man saw it more fit to embrace than to shun. A troublesome boy had received guidance as on his way to manhood and was now in a better position to become a useful member of society.

What legacy will you leave behind?

"And you yourself must be an example to them by doing good works of every kind. Let everything you do reflect the integrity and seriousness of your teaching." – Titus 2:9

CHAPTER 9

LEMONS HAVE SEEDS

There are two times of the year that lemons are sure to be in the refrigerator: the summer months and thanksgiving weekend. This cross between a sour orange and a citron might find its way on to the grocery list at other times when a specific recipe calls for it, but you can bet your grandma's locket that the summer heat and the thanksgiving dinner spread will see us reaching for the fruit.

"Why?", you ask?

I'll tell you why….

In the Fall of Samantha's 5th year, she somehow happened upon a recipe for lemon cookies. I cannot recall how or why she collided with that recipe, but she nagged for days for us to make the lemon cookies from the recipe. There was a lot going on in the house at the time, and we kept fending off the constant buffeting of the tenacious pint-sized old soul, not wanting to deal with the mess and confusion that would always accompany a family kitchen session. She did (finally) manage to back us into a corner, making us promise to take on the activity over the upcoming Thanksgiving holiday weekend. As the big day approached, we all had to go over the recipe (that she painstakingly copied off the internet, by hand, into her little notebook) and ensure that all the ingredients were accounted for. Samantha, in *true Samantha-style*, was leaving nothing to chance – we had to double check everything!

When the big day arrived, the adults quickly realized that they were going to be faced with the very thing they had tried to avoid. With all 6 of us in the kitchen, it was only a matter of time before everyone wanted the same spoon at the same time, and there was no way that another spoon could do the job of the spoon that the other person had. Soon someone was blocking someone else, nobody wanted to wait their turn with the measuring cup…. chaos was coming in like the tide on a full moon night. It was then that I had one of those rare moments of brilliance. "Why don't the mom and the girls work on the lemon cookies, since it was your idea (Samantha), while the boys and I make cornbread?", I suggested.

Daddy was the star of the show for the next hour or so!

That was a much more manageable plan and pretty soon each team was working out their own system and getting their assigned task done. The cornbread was a hit at dinner and desert (the cookies) was oh so scrumptious. Just like that, the SBs had established their Thanksgiving tradition!

As for lemon and the Summer, I'm afraid that story is a lot less inspired. We, just like many others, simply like to have lemonade when its hot. 😊

With the size of our family, we could easily go through a large pitcher of lemonade in a single sitting if the day is hot enough, especially if it is one of those times where I get the sugar-water-lemon juice measurements just right. I always seem to be tasked with making this cooling concoction because, apparently, "I'm the best at it". I know that when such compliments are given it is just flattery that is meant to protect them from their kick at the can, but I take it anyway – it feels good to be flattered. With that said though, I do look for opportunities to delegate at times, just so I don't come off as one who enjoys being played. If I'm going to make the drink then someone is going to juice the lemons and someone else is going to wash up when we're done. I don't mess around; I lay down the law! (It is rare that anyone actually listens to said law….but I lay it down anyway).

One of those rare times was on an afternoon where the sun decided to break its own record for heat production. I do not recall the particular temperature that we had to contend with on that day, but it was HOTTT!

I had set up the inflatable wading pool outside and the little ones were splashing about while Sophon, Shereece and I tried desperately to stay in the shade on the deck. I was whipping up a batch of lemonade, assisted by my unenthused sous chef (Shereece), when she made a comment about how many seeds was in the lemon she was working on. I don't know how Samantha, who was now 6 years old, heard the comment, or what inspired her to act in the way that she did, but she was out of the pool in a jiffy and by Shereece's side with her little arm outstretched, palm up.

"Give them to me", she demanded.

Shereece quizzically obliged, wondering what was going on in her little sister's head.

Clutching the seeds, she headed out into the yard, picked up a stick then started digging along the edge of the concrete landing. She would dig holes about 2 feet apart and plant a single seed until her hands were empty. Sophon and I exchanged glances, chuckling a little to ourselves, since we knew that the upcoming cold months would deny those seeds any chance of growth. Whether or not Samantha ever gave that reality a second thought is still to be known. What was apparent for days to come was her commitment to the cause, as she would be sure to water those seeds twice a day everyday until she forgot about them, like 6-year-olds tend to do.

I was well within my adult years before I started to realize the power that our thoughts have, and how our perception of things/circumstances dictate the way we approach them. The analogy of the proverbial glass being half-full (positive) or half-empty (negative) was not one that I fully embraced in my younger years since, regardless of how you look at it, the amount of liquid in the glass was always the same. However, the lemon-adage that encourages us to look at challenges as opportunities has helped me in many instances of my life. Turning lemons into lemonade, searching for the pot of gold at the end of rainbows, seeing the silver lining around clouds – I have almost become a master at it all. Sometimes annoyingly so (yes, I have actually been told that).

But Samantha took me a step further that summer afternoon and started me on another leg of my growth journey. By watching her take the seeds of this not-to-be-enjoyed-by-itself fruit and try to turn those seeds into a mini orchard, I realized that I am often the limiting factor in many of my challenging situations. If I am to resort to taking challenges, life's lemons, and turning them into pitchers of lemonade, I would be doing well as far as handling the situation and turning it into a positive experience. But looking for those seeds, the base object from which challenges come, and seeking ways to use those bases to change my surroundings and my future would be even better.

What do I mean? Allow me to give an example:

A lemon that has been tossed at me recently involves a strained and vexing work relationship. In this time where equality of the sexes is a not-so-silent battle that is raging on societal levels, the intensity of that battle is much more heightened on the professional front. Women who supervise men will laud it over them in covert (and sometimes overt) ways, and women who report to men are often more combative that they need to be, all in the name of being "strong, independent and equal". The workplace is tantamount to a WWII minefield on most days.

I stepped on one of those mines recently as I faced off with a disgruntled employee that I supervise. We had been peers for a while before my promotion, and she had always been dismissive and condescending to me, but my moving into a more superior position just exacerbated the contention. Now I could have wasted much time and energy trying to come up with a way to fix that specific relationship, but I realized that there was a need to go deeper than that. The truth is that the professional landscape is changing in such a way that we are seeing many more women achieving ranks of power. My direct supervisor is a woman and there are several other women that rank above her on the organization's totem pole. If I am to have any hope of excelling in this brave new world, I need to identify the root of the problem that I was having with this individual and work at it in such a way that it will help similar interactions in the future.

I have found that it is possible to employ that same principle to other areas of life. Friendships, intimate relationships, neighborly relations – they all have defining base points. By training my mind to see the basic elements that form the foundations of these interactions, I can become adept at identifying ways to enhance the relationships or fix difficulties when they arise. Becoming a master at making lemonade out of life's lemons is great, but it is more of a reaction and not an action. True mastery of life's happenings come when one is able to take proactive steps to set up future successes. When dealing with challenges, an isolated immediate fix can often limit future possibilities.

"And we know that God causes everything to work together for the good of those who love Him and are called according to His purpose."

– Romans 8:28

CHAPTER 10

PLANTED NOT BURIED

How many times have you heard the phrase, "If you work hard, your future will be without limits."? If I had a dollar for every time I heard those words, I would be in a much different circle than I am today.

Growing up, it seemed that this line was commonly repeated in the Teachers' lounge at my elementary school. Mrs. Scott, Ms. Barrett, Mrs. Tate, Ms. Dennie – every one of those ladies treated that statement like it was breathed by God himself. As young students, we were given no choice but to adopt such teachings if we were to have any hopes of passing through the grades and earning the right to march down the aisle with fellow graduands one day. These dedicated scholastic task masters would ensure their students had enough homework assignments to keep them away from any TV time their parents would want to allow. Couple these stalwarts of tutelage with hard-core Caribbean parents who never knew a life of ease, and you understand how 'hard work' was never in short supply for this little boy.

I was a sucker for it actually. As much as my hands were always full with schoolwork, somehow it still made sense for me to land a weekend job at age 12; a job that I would keep until I graduated from collegial studies some 9 years later. Throughout that whole time the benefits gained solely from my reputation as a good, consistent, and diligent worker opened many doors for me before I even arrived at the doorsteps. There were scholarships, sponsorships, and support commitments that were offered to my parents on my behalf and as I look back, I realize that I had every reason to become complacent.

Andy Grove, the Hungarian-American business Tycoon, reportedly shared his belief that 'success breeds complacency, and as a child/young adult, I was comparatively successful. I was never materially rich, but I was somehow able to consistently reach my goals (modest though they were), which became the dew that watered the tree of my confidence. Though somehow able to escape the clutches of self-absorption and arrogance, I was never scared to try, to reach, to dream, to aspire – because failure was not something that I was overly familiar with.

It wasn't until I migrated to Canada and landed my first job as a Sonographer that I was caused to question the validity of my childhood mantra. The work etiquette that had become second nature had earned me the respect of my peers, the confidence of my direct superiors, and the trust of my patients. My name was being spoken of (in a good way) in circles that I was never present in, and in those instances when my name wasn't known, it was still quite easy for descriptions to point in my direction. Afterall, I was one of three men on the Ultrasound team at the time, and the only black person of the more than 100 employees of the facility. It was, indeed, quite difficult to confuse me with another.

One of my fondest professional memories will forever be that Tuesday morning after my second son was born. My wife had just valiantly brough child number 4 into the world 2 days before and, now having gotten the green light from the midwife, we were bringing him home to meet his siblings. As I wheeled my heroine and my brand-new prince, meandering the maze that was the hospital hallways, I happened upon one of the doctors with whom I worked talking to one of his physician colleagues. We stopped and exchanged pleasantries, giving me the opportunity to proudly show off my new son (as if I had that much to do with him being there). As I introduced the portion of my family that was present, he in turn introduced me to his colleague by saying, "This is Sheldon. He is the best Ultrasound Tech that I have ever worked with".

I don't know if it was me receiving such praise by a respected consultant Obstetrician, or if it was that the praise of a respected Obstetrician was being offered in the presence of my wife (that's a huge deal – let me tell you), but that was a day of days for me. I always knew I was good, I was always heard I was good, but to go down in his book as "the best he's ever worked with"?!

I felt a serious sense of pride in that moment! Judge me all you want but that was a big day for me.

The days that followed saw me ruminating on those words, bouncing from cloud to cloud. But the question eventually presented itself: if what he said is true, how then am I at the same place that I started 5 years ago? Five years on the frontline, passed over for more than a couple promotions, and earning just over $2 per hour more than when I first began? There was something wrong with that picture for me.

I had worked hard, I had kept my head down, I had done everything right, but the leadership at my place of employment seemed intent on keeping me from rising. As I reviewed and evaluated the years leading up to that moment it became clear to me that my place in the ranks was by design. There was never any interest from management to help me develop professionally, to help me rise. And every time I availed myself to an opening that would elevate my position, there was always someone else 'more fitting' for the job.

I wasn't angry. I wasn't bitter. But it hurt.

It hurt enough for me to confide in another member of the team who had taken on the role of a mentor to me in the months leading up to that time. *George and I would share many moments in his office and on the phone talking about my professional aspirations and the challenges that stood in the way of realizing them. He understood because he had fought similar battles in his younger professional years. Even at his stage of life, he was still having to navigate unfriendly waters in the very same place that I worked, leading us to become kindred spirits. I don't know if he would ever ascribe any personal benefit to our time together, but I know that I reaped a lot from speaking and listening to him. George opened my eyes to pathways that would help me build on what I have been able to accomplish and escape the professional prison to which I had somehow been sentenced.

We've since lost touch, but I truly hope that I will get the chance to one day look George in the eye and shake his hand one more time. It is not everyday that growth comes from despair, but there is never a day that it isn't possible.

He showed me that!

I don't much care for birds. They're nice and all, but I don't go crazy for them the way my wife does. Yes, I put up the birdhouses and buy birdseeds, but that's more for a peaceful life than anything else. It is for that reason that I was so nonchalant last spring when there were grumblings in the house about the squirrel that was eating all the sunflower seeds that were put out for the birds. I didn't see what the big fuss was about.

"Live and let live", was my thinking!

We refilled the birdfeeders a couple of times, and the seeds would disappear much faster than we expected. We knew it wasn't the birds eating that many that quickly. It turned out that we had a furry little enemy who lived in the tree on the property line who was making full use of our hospitality. It wasn't until later in the summer that his actions were betrayed.

One afternoon as my wife was out pulling some weeds, she noticed some new sprouts that "didn't quite look like weeds". As much as she isn't a professional florist, this insightful woman had a knack for differentiating between good and bad plants just by their leaves, stem thickness, depth of color, angle of growth (ok, I'm stretching the last one a little bit), but she just always seemed to know what a weed looked like. I learned long ago not to argue where that was concerned.

So, when she called me over to look at these sprouts that she could not recall planting, I accepted that it was something most peculiar. We agreed to let them grow and reveal their true colors in time. Imagine my surprise when, after pulling into the driveway one afternoon, my daughter came running up to me, yelling that mommy needed me in the backyard right away. Had it not been for the grin across her little face I would have been sure that someone was dying back there. I made my way over to where the garden bed was and let my gaze follow where my wife's finger was pointing.

There, down in the dirt among her begonias, were some budding miniature sunflowers. Her excitement quickly became my excitement since sunflowers – all variations – are my all-time favorite flowers. I am not one to gush over the beauty of roses or tulips; I prefer plants that feed me (give me mango trees any day). But sunflowers have a special place in my heart for some reason and she knew this. We looked at each other and smiled….for a while. Over the next few weeks, we would be blessed with a nice grove of sunflowers that we did not plant, and I am willing to bet that when *Mr Furry Face* had hidden and buried those seeds, he had no idea that they would one day grow and bloom. He might have thought he was strengthening his stores and protecting his own selfish interests. Little did he know that those seeds would one day defy his efforts and rise above the limits he had set for them.

I think back and I remember how I was downtrodden and buried; how more energy was put into holding me back than letting me grow. I smile. Apparently it is true what they say, "sometimes when others think you're being buried, you're only being planted". Hindrances have a way of hurting in the moment, and no one can deny that. We don't enjoy being held back or held down. But a resilient mindset – one that embraces inner strength and identifies avenues to manifest that strength – will make all the difference in the outcome of those situations. Defeat is only final if it is allowed to be.

"*But Thanks Be to God! He gives us the victory through the Lord Jesus Christ.*"– 1 Corinthians 15:57

CHAPTER 11

TINY HOLE, BIG PROBLEM

If you've been married for more than 5 years, then you've probably been through it. If you've been married for less than 5 years, be prepared for it. If you've never been married……never mind.

"The 5-year Itch" is a term coined by marriage experts to describe that point in a marriage when things start to fall apart. With the honey-moon phase long gone by then, and real-life (complete with a baby or two) now front and center, many married couples begin to lose their affinity for the relationship and start to think more frequently about what 'life out there' could be for them. It used to be called 'the 7 year itch' but that number has since been reduced to 5, which is indicative of the rate at which marriages are crumbling today. The good news, according to these experts, is that couples who make it past this point in their marriage will typically go on to have a long and fulfilling life together since they would have developed the necessary tools for marital longevity within those critical early years.

While intentionally side-stepping the marriage aspect of the conversation, I will admit that I have met this itch on several occasions from a professional standpoint. Every 4 – 5 years I start to think about and look for that next step; that next move. Again, this falls within the information provided by 'the experts' as it has been declared that average tenure of an employee is around 5 years. Whether or not they are just blowing smoke is questionable since I am yet to make it to the 6-year mark at any one job since graduating college.

I remember the days when changing jobs, which would often mean changing my home address, was nothing but exciting. As a bachelor, I could pack a single suitcase, call up a friend with a truck that can fit my 3 pieces of furniture, and be done with the whole move in an afternoon. The prospect of moving a new city, to make new friends, discover new restaurants, drive new roads brought such excitement to me. But I have come to realize that it is an extremely different experience when you add family to the mix. The process of finding a house takes on a whole new complexion when the decisions are split between what you want and what you are being told that you want. Then there is the search for a good school for the kids and assessing the practicality of commuting to and from that school. Are there parks or playgrounds nearby? How far is the library from home? Does the house have a yard? Does the yard have a fence? Does the fence have gates?

The simplicity of the bachelor's process becomes a distant and faded memory real fast.

But of all the relocations that we have been through as a family, I think the most recent one was the most exciting!

My ambitious pursuits, prodded on by the intrepid dreamer who is my *sweetie-pie* saw me landing a job that was 4,000 km from our home of 7 years. The whole thing had taken us by surprise and, to be honest, we 'talked lovingly' about it for a while before agreeing to move. But once we did, we were all in! There were grand plans of buying an acreage property and building our dream home, creating our own little piece of paradise where the kids could grow up closer to nature and have space and freedom to explore safely. While I spearheaded the search for the perfect piece of land, my wife got to work designing the house with such detail that the builders we consulted were all sure that the drawings were done by someone with professional training. My wife…..the science/chemistry buff…..had them all fooled. My chest would puff up with pride every time the question was asked though.

As we searched and dreamed and drew and dreamed and re-drew…and dreamed, we also found time to watch every home-steading video there was online. When I say we were all in, I mean we were all in! I had even found the perfect used RV that we could live in on our land and watch our home go up. It was a pretty large unit – 32 feet with a front queen bedroom and a rear bunkhouse that would sleep 4. The huge slide-out with a dinette and pull-out couch faced the well-equipped kitchen. It was just downright perfect, even though the purchase price made us stretch a little bit. Since I had gone ahead of the family to start the job, I handled all the arrangements and booked us a long-term spot at a campground where we could stay while we worked on the land purchase. It took some doing, but things went along pretty well and in due time we were all settled in our trailer at the campground and ready to take on our new adventure.

Within days we were made to realize just how big a battle we had taken on. The 32 feet that was massive in the beginning disappeared real fast as soon as the kids woke up. 3 of the 4 kids got up with the sun and 2 of the early risers considered it a cardinal sin to sit still. On bright sunny days when they could go outside and play, we felt hopeful. Rainy days brought us close to tears….every time. My wife did all she could to hide her struggle with the situation (bless her heart) and she did it very well, until we ran into problems with the black-tank's plumbing, forcing us to make alternate toilet arrangements and spending a small fortune on air fresheners. One look in her eyes and I got the message loud and clear! I called Nick, our realtor, and politely asked him to refocus his energy from finding us a 'vacant property' to a 'move-in-ready' house with an option for quick occupancy.

Nick was a friend, a church brother, and an all-around great guy. But in that moment, all I needed him to be was a phenomenal realtor and he came through splendidly on that front. Within 5 weeks we had found a house, negotiated the purchase, jumped through every hoop possible to secure financing, and were ready to move into a place where we could manage to turn around in the shower. We got in just before the winter conditions came upon us - a little deflated, but relieved. We had a really nice home with a yard, the kids were all happy and comfortable, and an RV that we would look to sell in the Spring, since 32ft was a little too big to be dragging around from one campground to the next. At least we would be able to get that money back.

The following May came soon enough and we started to think about summer fun. First on our list was to replace the RV with a more travel-friendly version. I cleaned it up, listed it on Facebook and smiled as the queries came through in a flood. Within a couple of days, we had a few interested buyers, and eventually there was one who made downpayment. On the morning that he was to come to collect his prize and pay the remainder of the purchase price, I went out to do one last recon and saw water dripping through the ceiling of the front bedroom. If you listened closely you would have heard my heart hit the floor. The more I checked along the roof and the walls, the more my stomach churned and my insides knotted. From inside the RV you could tell that the entire front-end of the unit was rotten. I was in shock! How could this be? It was perfectly fine when we parked last Fall!

Grabbing a ladder, I climbed up to take a look from the outside and sure enough, there along the seal was a ~2-inch gap in the rubber seal. I tried to reseal that area, but it was too late. The entire front clip had a visibly *wavy* contour, shouting to the world that the elements had beaten us soundly. An entire winter's worth of snow was once piled on top of the unit, and as that snow melted, a good bit of the resulting water found its way into that 2-inch gap. We still managed to sell the unit, but it took a lot of doing and we lost a fair bit of money in the end.

We still talk about that whole experience, gleefully reminiscing at times, complaining bitterly at other times. Through it all though, I can certainly say that my family now readily submits to the intricacies of RV ownership – especially the importance of a good winter cover.

I have heard it said the human eye can detect the light of a candle from approximately 2 miles away. That, in and of itself, is simply awesome. But rather than focusing on the ability of the eye in this scenario, I want to highlight the effect of the single candle flame. True, the light from that candle will offer no real guidance to the observer from 2 miles away. But take away that light from the equation with all other variables remaining, and there would be nothing on the horizon for the superb human eye to detect. There would only be pure, unadulterated, darkness.

Little things can have huge impacts - a truth that is often not accepted or applied as often as it should be. Small moments of indiscretion can have life-long impacts.

I can recall multiple instances where my mother preached to me about the dangers of leaving my mind open to impure influences. Like most youth, I went through the phase where music was my life; some would say I am still in that phase on most days. I would meander my way from genre to genre and, as embarrassing as it is to admit, there was a time when hardcore rap was my go-to music, especially after I started driving. I mean, it was hard to lean the seat way back, put my sunglasses on, and look cool with Celine Dion blaring from my speakers. The issue though was that while other genres had the odd ‘ bad song’, rap music of my day tended to have the odd 'good song', and my mother was rightfully concerned about the effects of such things on her boy.

I fought her tooth-and-nail back then, but now I find myself repeating her words to my children almost on a daily basis. Guarding the mind is of infinite importance since it is the mind that defines who we are. The books we read, the music we listen to, the movies we watch, they all have an impact on our mind and are therefore helping to shape who we are at every turn. Let no one take the position that they are unaffected by 'harmless' pastimes. One cannot unhear that which is heard or unsee whatever is seen. The man or woman, boy or girl, who seeks to be their best selves will do all they can to guard their mind.

Do not be fooled. The type of destruction that came to a 32ft RV because of a 2-inch gap can also reach the most brilliant but loosely guarded mind.

"Guard your [mind] above all else, for it determines the course of your life."
(Proverbs 4:23)

CHAPTER 12

BIKING 101

Blame deferral! It is so very difficult to find a more prevalent human trait than this.

It is so much easier, and almost innate, for someone to point fingers when things don't go as planned or desired. Children blame the dog for eating their homework, teens blame the media for their 'undesirable tendencies', and adults blame their upbringing for their shortcomings. This tendency is widely accepted as a coping mechanism designed to provide an escape from guilty conscience. If the fault is not yours, then you are not liable or culpable.

Well, my son, in a very round-about way, brought this issue to life for me in a way that has never left me.

On this particular Thursday afternoon, the whole family ditched the indoors and took all the bikes outside. The kids were still pretty young, which meant Sophon and I would be walking as the others worked on their cycling skills. The youngest was 2yrs old at the time so he was most often in a stroller during these sessions, while our older son, Shemar, and younger daughter, Samantha, had training wheels on their two-wheelers. Now Samantha, much like her older sister Shereece, had an uncanny ability to excel at any and everything that she tried. At the time, her balance was still not where it was going to be months down the road, but she had a firm grip on maneuvering her bike and she loved showing off just how good she was at it.

She would go flying by at break-neck speeds on her little pink machine, tassels flying off the handlebars, ringing her bell, grinning from ear to ear. I would watch her in amazement while Sophon would be having a heart attack. But she was hell-bent on enjoying every moment of her childhood. Shemar, on the other hand, found himself in a bit of a conundrum.

His little blue racer was not cooperating. He was doing everything he saw his sister doing, but he was not having as much fun as she was. As I silently watched him that afternoon, I could almost hear him ticking off the boxes in his head:

- Sit on the bike = CHECK!
- Hold the handle-bars = CHECK!
- Put my feet on the pedals = CHECK!
- Look ahead = CHECK!

…and then he would sit there, waiting, expecting….wondering why he wasn't moving!

Time and time again he would look down at his feet, look down on the ground, twist the handlebars, furrow his brow…..trying desperately to identify the piece of the puzzle that was missing. He came off the bike, knelt down beside it and stared at the wheels, re-mount the bike, and go through the checklist again. Still – no luck! His bike just wasn't kicking up dust like his sister's was.

By now my wife is almost in stitches while I am struggling to keep a straight face. We were having way too much fun at his expense, kicking ourselves for not getting it all on camera.

It didn't take much longer before he came off the bike, threw his hand in the air and hollered, "It's not working!"

Playing the genuinely caring and oh-so-understanding father role, I went over to my bewildered son and enquired, "what's not working, son?"

That invitation was the perfect opportunity for my prince to blame the bike for not doing what Samantha's bike was doing. The bike was broken! By this time, Samantha had taken a break from her riding and was at the nearby playground. Shemar jumped at the opportunity and, racing over to her bike, jumped on it with great excitement. This was the bike that works! He just saw it work for his sister, so now he's sure it will work for him! Maybe I should have stopped him. Perhaps that's what a great father would do to spare their child from the heartache of disappointment, but, sadly, I lost the nomination for father of the year in that moment. I watched him run over, climb on, and go through his mental checklist again…..and then it was if I could hear his heart shatter. This bike was now broken too!

He was almost to tears by the time I got to his side. It just wasn't fair that everything worked for Samantha, and nothing worked for him. In his mind he was doing exactly what he saw her and every other child around him doing, so what was his curse? What was it that was so wrong with him that caused bikes to just break whenever he attempted to use them?

Sophon and I spent a good chunk of the rest of the afternoon trying to explain the importance of pedaling to our deflated son. He hadn't noticed before that the other young biker's feet were moving when they went sailing by. His little mind had just assumed that those were footrests designed to keep your feet from dragging in the dirt. You could see the lightbulb go on when we raised the rear wheel and showed him how the turning of the pedals set the wheel into motion. He could barely contain himself when he recognized that his bike wasn't broken after all. He only needed to push the pedals.

Seeing him come back from the brink of the emotional abyss was such an uplifting experience. Every parent, regardless of whether they are well-experienced or if they are new to the whole parenting thing, can attest to the joy that is felt when they get to teach their child something and see that child accept it. The super-parenting-duo had done it again, and we stepped back to give the youngster the space to show us what he had learned.

With a wide grin he jumped back on his bike, assumed the position and began to pedal…..backwards.

Oh boy!……

There is a saying that goes, "education is the key to success", but many forget that a key will only reveal its maximum value when mated with its designated lock. The same truth underlines many other aspects of life. Knowledge is of very little value if it isn't used appropriately, talent will not pay dividends if it remains buried, and opportunities will always pass by if interested parties do not seek to take advantage of them. Success, in any of its forms, demands that effort be made. Success and fulfillment require definite and intentional action.

Blame games, while quite effective at making us feel good about ourselves, is one sure way to limit our potential. Not being honest enough with ourselves to critically assess our own behaviors, actions, or inactions will always result in us not being able to move ahead in our journey. There are certainly times when other people or surrounding circumstances are at fault, and we should never be afraid to speak up in such cases. But the man or woman who somehow always seems to end up being the victim should take a long, hard look at themselves. It is quite likely that these introspective sessions will reveal more than a few instances where unfortunate outcomes were more the results of one's own missteps than they were externally engendered.

If, the focus lies on looking the part, then sitting on the bike with your feet on the pedal will do just fine. Should there be a desire to move from point A to point B however, then the pedals must be pushed, and the wheels be made to turn. Intentional, calculated efforts must be made. Hopes, dreams, and desires alone will never be enough to reach a goal. Taking ownership of the process and putting in the work remains an absolute necessity.

"*Whatever you do, work at it with all your heart…*" – Colossians 3:23

CHAPTER 13

Grab A Shovel

As an island boy growing up, I was always fascinated by the snow. As much as I could not fully grasp how people could live in a place where it was cold enough for ice to exist outside of a freezer for months on end, I was still enthused by the winter sports that I saw on the many television shows.

Of course, it was all romanticized. Based on what I saw in the movies, everyone was born with a natural talent for skiing, snowboarding, and ice-skating – it seemed to be second nature. They made it seem like there was no need for special equipment or training if you wanted to ski. You simply slapped one some long flat slats, lean forward, and let gravity take you down the hillside in style. James bond and Xander Cage (enviable TV personas) were proof that anyone could do it! As for driving on the white stuff?....there was absolutely no need to be concerned about that part; cars basically corrected themselves as you slid around corners.

To my mind, those folks living in parts of the USA and all of Canada had life easy. They didn't have to deal with the torrential rainstorms and hurricanes that us islanders had to worry about. If ever I got the chance to live where there was snow, I was going to enjoy every bit of it! That would be a welcomed difference!

Well, I live in Canada now, and if James Bond or Xander cage were to show up on my doorstep today, I would:

1. Slap them…….really hard…….for all their trickery
2. Apologize for slapping them and beg to be spared their almighty wrath
3. Whine about my torn rotator cuff that I got from my first (and only) attempt at ice skating
4. Complain bitterly about the prohibitive costs of good skiing equipment (even though that is really not their fault, but why not…)
5. Ask where I can get a hidden grappling installed on my care that could save me from sure death should I spin out (again) in the snow

Ok, fine…..you're right. Maybe I wouldn't do any of that.

But there is no arguing with me about the stark contrast between assumptions and reality, and one reality that hit me really hard really quickly, is how difficult shoveling snow can be.

My first experience with shoveling snow wasn't even for myself. I was living in London, Ontario at the time in my second year as an international student. It was the Saturday morning that followed 2 days of non-stop snowfall – the first such snowstorm that I had witnessed at that point. I got up, like I do on Saturday mornings, and got dressed to go to church. I was a lowly student in a strange city with no friends, and that meant that my only option for travel was to take the city bus.

I got on the bus, grabbed a window seat and settled in for the 45 min ride to my destination. As the bus made its way through the neighbourhoods, I found myself watching people digging themselves out. I chuckled to myself as I passed this one house that seemed to have a mile-long driveway. That dude was sure to be sore by the end of the day.

But then I saw her.

She was a small elderly woman, no more than 5 feet tall and easily in her 70's. She was out there chipping away at the ice that the city's snow-removal truck had left at the entrance to her driveway. Don't ask me why (because I couldn't tell you) but as if by reflex I hit the 'request stop' button in the bus, asking to be let off at the next bus stop – which just happened to be about 2 houses down from where the woman was. Something in me was uncomfortable with seeing her bent over in the negative temperatures, doing her best to challenge this mound of ice that blocked the entrance to her home. She saw me approaching (I know this because we made eye contact) but she was still visibly shocked when I stopped and offered to help her with her chore. Not only was I a stranger, but I was a well-dressed stranger clutching a bible, and it didn't take a genius to figure out that I didn't know what I was getting into. My slippery dress shoes and woefully inadequate mittens were dead giveaways. I may not have been dressed for the job, but she knew she was not up to the challenge at hand either.

We exchanged pleasantries before she handed over her shovel to me. She lived alone but was expecting her daughter and family to visit for the weekend. Her house was right on the street, so if she didn't have the driveway cleared by the time they arrived, then they would have nowhere safe to park. She was trying to make sure her grandkids were not forced to challenge the traffic as they entered or exited their parents' vehicle. I smiled. She was too sweet.

Well then, I traded my bible for her shovel and got ready to make quick work of this driveway.

Now I should point out here that prior to this episode, my only experience with shovels was digging holes for my mom to plant stuff. Or perhaps to move some sand when my dad was taking on some job around the house. Nobody told me that shoveling snow required a whole different technique.

My first dig at the snow/ice combo sent a shock through my wrists all the way down to the L4 vertebra in my spine. I wanted to drop the shovel, grab my bible and chase after the bus that had just passed by. I had no idea which bus that was, where it was coming from, or where it was going, but I was willing to enter through the window if it meant escaping this punishment that I signed up for.

How could the light fluffy stuff that floats ever so gently down from the sky be so heavy?? I just couldn't fathom it! To make matters worse, it would appear that the basal layers of the snowfall had melted and refroze to create a hardened substrate that was well hidden by its softer lighter covering.

In that moment I realized the wisdom that I had seen, and ridiculed, just the day before.

I had sat in the room that I was renting and looked out the window to see my neighbors out there shoveling their driveways. I was a renter, which meant snow removal was my landlord's job and was included in the rent. But I saw these people shoveling the snow even as it was snowing. "That's just foolish", I thought.

Why not just wait until its all done, then clear it once and for all? Shoveling during the storm is just a waste of energy and time.

Well, even though I know the limitations of my new 'friend', I was silently wishing she had been shoveling for the two days prior. That driveway took every bit of wind and pride out of me. I slipped more than a few times, I almost flat-out fell once, my shoes were no longer spotless, and the armpits of my shirt were shouting to the world about the intensity of this laborious undertaking. Nevertheless, my pride and my parents' upbringing kept me from walking away from this dame-in-distress who was clearly in need. I stuck it out till the end, and I smiled a big smile when I moved the last shovel-full of the white stuff from her doorway.

We never exchanged names or numbers, and I never saw or spoke to her again. I don't know what became of her daughter's visit, or even if the daughter did visit. But as I walked into church to catch the last 10 mins of the service that Saturday morning, I was convicted of two things:

1. There are people all around who need help and most of them will never ask for it.
2. I needed better winter gloves.

When dealing with challenges, there is often the tendency to give up or quit when there doesn't seem to be any evidence of change, and that's understandable. I mean, really – why keep trying when all of your efforts are seemingly fruitless? What sense is there in working at a problem when it seems to only get harder with each passing day?

Well, the 'dumb' neighbors who kept shoveling even as the snow was piling up around them demonstrated one response to those questions. To the uninitiated, it was absolutely nonsensical to keep shoveling when you know that the path you just cleared will be full again in seconds. But if they had chosen to wait until the snow stopped to attempt removal, the task would have been much greater, and even close to insurmountable for some (like my little old friend).

Continuing to try, even when things don't seem to be improving, is not necessarily senseless. More often than not, this manifestation of one's intrepid nature is a sign of hopeful foresight. That which is done here and now will make the demands of the future a lot more manageable. Waiting until the skies clear can sometimes leave you with a bigger problem than you'd like.

The truth is that the storm will always end…..always! How much of the aftermath that you are left to deal with depends on what you were doing during the storm.

"And let us not grow weary of doing good, for in due season we will reap, if we do not give up."

- Galatians 6:9

CHAPTER 14

GOODBYE APPLE PIE

"If a man says he's gonna fix it, he's gonna fix it! There's no need to remind him every three months."

I saw that quote on a t-shirt once and I could hardly hold back the chuckle that resulted. Not only was I impressed by the generally inherent truth of the statement, I also wondered who exactly it was that decided to be my hero and defend my honor so valiantly. Let me be clear here: I am not a pathological procrastinator by any means. In fact, one of the complaints that I get from my Better Half quite frequently is that I tend to be.....impulsive. I am inclined to describe that virtue differently, choosing to see myself as a person who is able to critically assess a situation, evaluate multiple possible outcomes, and choose the option that is likely to fail with impressive speed. Said decisions may not always lead to the place I said they would, but hey - can't win them all, right?

However, when it comes to projects that require intense manual labor, tasks that are likely to cause me to perspire and markedly increase my heart rate, I have been known to give snails a good name.

I….take…my…time! I need to plan!

Take the fencing of our yard, for example. When we bought our third home, we liked everything about the property. Sophon had nearly no complaints about the house (other than the front of the house not being positioned to face the morning sun), and though I instantly recognized that my lawn-mowing time had just tripled when compared to our previous home, I was happy that the kids would have ample space to frolic. The one apprehension that we both had was that the yard was only fenced on two sides.

I didn't dare bring up what I was thinking initially – a man's gotta be smart about such things. I followed her lead and surveyed our new estate, watching the kids running around without abandon, giving the time and space needed to let things happen organically. It wasn't long before I heard the question I had been waiting for: "do you think you could finish the fencing for the yard?". I felt like I had just won the lottery, but I wasn't about to appear too eager. I placed my hand to my chin, let out a few 'hmms', and then calmly responded, "let me look into it.". Having just sold our previous home where I had built the kids their very own playset in the backyard, complete with a 3-station swing, and a mini-house with a balcony and a slide, I was all confident and excited to take on another building project.

You may ask, "why so much excitement"?

And to that I would offer the simple mathematical explanation:

Proposed home project + wife's blessing = a sanctioned set of **NEW TOOLS!**

Yep! I was going to need a new air compressor (a big one), a pneumatic nail gun, a new drill with multiple batteries, a mitre saw, and a table saw. I was going to have to make several trips to the local Home Depot and shop in the Contractors aisle where all the other 'manly men' hang out. I felt like a 10yr old kid who had just been gifted an all-expense paid trip to Disney land. The only problem was that this was September, and September is not the time to start yard projects in Canada. It was decided that the project would wait until the following Spring, which gave me all of 6 months of wintery conditions to study and prepare.

Well, that sounded like a good plan at the time. But it turns out that the extended down-time was like a big bucket of cold water on my blazing fire. By the time October was done, I had watched every video there was to watch on YouTube and I was as close to a fencing expert as I was ever going to be. But, sadly, I couldn't carry that momentum all the way into the following May/June when the ground would have thawed sufficiently for me to dig the post holes. The 6 month pause on the project has turned into almost 3 years as I write these words, which is embarrassing if I am to be completely honest.

It hasn't been a total loss though. Our children have been remarkably good at staying in the backyard as they play, not venturing out into the street. And other than dealing with the neighbour's dog who thinks it is OK to declare our yard his personal toilet, it has been a largely uneventful fenceless living. Added to that is the blessing of some enviable happenings over the years. Time and time again all 6 of us within the house would huddle by the dining room window to watch 'the neighbourhood moose' eat from the trees in our yard. He would sleep in the yard and do his part to help keep the trees in check – making sure to leave me piles of 'his special gift' to clean up the next day. But he wasn't the only 'visitor from the wild to' stake claim to our slice of paradise. As parents, we had to be extra vigilant during the Fall and Spring months when bears go on their eating binge. Though we only had the skittish and shy black bears in our region, common sense still dictated that we watch out when any member of the family went outside, especially after dark.

This was one of the (very) good reasons that I protested and resisted planting any fruit trees in our yard. Along the way, Sophon had purchased a young potted apple tree from an acquaintance and tasked me with putting it into the ground. Though I simply couldn't be bothered to dig the large hole that the 6-foot apple tree required, the argument that I presented was that we didn't need to offer any more incentives for the bears to come into our space and endanger our sweet helpless little angels. We needed to keep things simple for our safety! In retrospect, that argument was not as wholesome as it could have been, since it only led to the tree staying in a pot RIGHT NEXT TO the house – closer to us than it would have been if I had planted it in the ground. And to add insult to injury, the doggone thing was so healthy that it eventually begun blossoming and bearing apples. Many of the apples didn't make it to maturity, but some did. Day by day my wife would go to the tree to observe the formation of the first fruits, and they were looking quite lovely.

As Fall progressed it came down to only 3 promising fruits, the mistress of the house had great plans for those three fruits. She was going to turn them into an apple pie – and I wasn't mad at the idea. Though I am generally one for salty snacks over sweet treats, I am helpless when it comes to a warm homemade goodie from the oven. For that reason, I joined her in hoping that those apples would ripen before the frost comes.

The days came and went until the time for harvest arrived. I had refrained from picking the apples myself as I felt it was only fair that she gets to reap the first fruits of her single-tree orchard. I offered the occasional reminder to her from time to time, but there was always a legitimate reason to put off the momentous event that should be executed with as much pomp and circumstance as possible. It turns out that she had wanted the kids to be the ones to pick the fruit, and to get a picture of the occasion for the photo banks. I would remind her in the morning, and she would commit to picking them at lunchtime when the kids had a break from their studies. Lunchtime would come and my follow-up reminder would be met with a promise for later that afternoon when they get back from their extracurricular activities. Before we knew it, another autumn day passed into history, leaving us exchanging harmless jabs at each other about our procrastinating ways. There was always a plan to redeem ourselves the following day.

But that was not to be.

One morning, we were greeted by the site of the apple tree lying on its side, by the house, all 3 of the apples gone. A large pile of fruity dung by the toppled tree told the tale of a hungry bear who had passed by while we slept. It would seem like such a small thing to most people, but we were devastated! My wife was almost in tears as she thought of how many opportunities we missed, only to lose it all in the end. If she had just took the few steps yesterday to go outside and grab the three perfectly ripened and unblemished orbs of juicy goodness, she would have been smiling happily in the kitchen instead of bridling the anger she was now feeling for that unwelcomed beast. I too was heart broken. Not only was My Love in pain, at the brink of tears, and beyond the reach of my help, but we weren't going to be having any apple pie on that day…..and that hurt!

How dare that bear?! Who did he (or she) think they were to just rob a man of his apple pie like that? If I could have gotten my hand on that creature in the moment, he would have been a rug by the next day. But we just had to nurse our wounds, place the tree back in its upright position, and crawl back inside.

The tree still stands outside in its pot, completely bare, waiting on Spring's wake-up call. Each time I am made to walk by it, I remember how close we came, and how quickly I lost my pie. I will never forgive that fake Yogi bear! Never!

We, as humans, have a tendency to equate progress with huge accomplishments. Incremental gains are readily dismissed and nullified because they do not produce some sort of earth shattering or obvious change. Subscription to such schools of thought will leave one forever doubting their value to their spouse, to their colleagues, to their organization, and to this world in general. The truth is that we all will not accomplish ground-breaking feats in our lifetime. I know – to many that sounds like a sad truth, but it is in fact a 'freeing' truth!

Why?

Because the moment we accept that progress is not defined by impact, we begin to realize that each and every intentional act that we execute is worthy of recognition. Please understand, here, that this is not an advocation for mediocrity. Far from it! Settling for what comes and accepting only what is given to you is not progressive. Progress comes when one achieves what they set out to do – whether in totality, or in increments.

Take the neighbourhood Black Bear for example. The seasonal clock of these large and powerful creatures dictate that they go into a coma of sorts for the entire winter season. Humans could never think to attempt what these bears do. Most people have great difficulty going for a single day without food, but these bears go for months without eating or drinking. To do this, they have to bulk up considerably in the months leading up to their hibernation. It is this bulk that breaks down slowly over the course of their deep sleep to keep them nourished and hydrated until the seasons change and their natural food sources revive.

They try to eat as much as they can while they can, but they don't limit themselves only to opportunities where a buffet is presented. They do not go around seeking the most heavily fruit-laden trees, ignoring the scraps that they may come across along the way. To them, every mouthful is a victory, and every swallow is important. It might only be three apples, but those will be three more apples than the bear had before, and it will be three less that need to be found.

Our journey through life will not always be blessed with fruit-laden trees of opportunity. There may be days when the only success is getting through the day with your sanity intact, or you may need to endure a scholastic journey that was to be 3 years in length but end up taking twice as long because circumstances require the alternating of study and hustle semesters. Do not scoff at these things and do not allow anyone to devalue them! Gather the apples that present themselves along the way. They may not represent the ideal, but they count towards the final goal.

The trick is to make sure that you know what aligns with your goal and what does not. A passive collection of anything and everything that comes along can be more detrimental than to your dream than you can imagine. The bear came into the yard on a mission: to find food. He was not there to collect bedding for his cave, nor was he there to looking for a toy. Even though all of those things were present in the backyard as he wandered around (my kids simply refuse to pack up their toys after play), the focus was on food for the winter ahead. The apple tree itself – the producer of the food that was needed - did not appeal to him. The singular focus of the moment were the apples. The amount of food was unimportant, but it had to be food to be important.

Great care should be taken to protect against enshrining the unimportant. Action or execution is not always towards a positive outcome. Progress is progress only when it is progressive.

"But as for you, be strong and do not give up, for your work will be rewarded." – 2 Chron 15:7

CHAPTER 15

WHEN STRONG WINDS BLOW

We had a lovely Summer, but it was now over.

Whenever anyone says they had a 'good summer', it usually means that they had a busy summer. That was no less true for us. This year we logged over 2,000 km of road trips, visiting family, connecting with old friends, and making new ones. The children even got to go to the local city fair for the first time! It was all around a great few months.

But the absolute high point of the entire season was the August day that we picked up our new travel trailer. She was brand new, a true beauty – the fruit born from years of wishing and months of searching. We had made the 7-hour trip to pick her up (yes, my wife is that specific about what she wants) and came back home without incident. We even got to sneak in two fun-filled camping trips in this *tricked-out-home-away-from-home* before the return of the school year put a hard stop to all such undertakings.

Now, with the temperatures changing, there was no denying that it was time to get all the winterizing done – and top of my list was to get a good trailer cover to keep the winter snow off this ridiculously expensive purchase. A we discussed in a previous chapter, a past painful and expensive experience had taught me the dangers of leaving these potential money pits exposed to that beautiful but angry side of mother nature. Winter in Canada is no joke, even worse so in Northern BC!

So yes, today was the day. The brown cardboard box on my front porch testified that Amazon had been faithful to their promise and had delivered my trailer cover right on time. The following Sunday morning I headed out to prepare *Sonic the Trailer* (the name assigned by my brood), for her Winter hibernation. Armed with bottles of antifreeze, the necessary tools, and the RV cover, I opened the door to the backyard only to stop in my tracks and let out a big sigh. There I stood on the back deck looking over my once-green lawn, now absolutely covered by dead, yellow and brown leaves, interspersed with a few twigs and pine needles.

That's the problem with Fall – it breaks the rhythm of summer and heralds the struggles of winter, all while adding the most mundane of tasks to the To-Do list. Maybe it was because raking leaves was my weekly chore growing up. Or maybe its because I find bagging leaves in the wind – a wind that always seems to come at that exact moment when I open the garbage bag – to be a most frustrating task. I can't quite put my finger on a singular reason, but I find raking leaves to be almost infuriating.

Based on past experience, I knew that what I was staring at in that moment was a warning that I had a tough evening ahead of me. I rolled my eyes and headed off to do my winterizing. I would get to those leaves when I'm good and ready – not a moment sooner.

Well, there I was, over an hour later, still trying to finish up with the trailer. YouTube and I typically work well together, and I thought I had the 'antifreeze' portion of the job down to a science. That was before I realized how well hidden the hot water tank was in this unit and how much the manufacturer had tightened the drain plug in that contraption. I choose to believe that the plug was machine-tightened. The thought of there being a man capable of producing that much torque with his bare hands somehow made me feel inadequate. I took solace in believing that the 45 mins it took to loosen that plug was all due to a mechanical arm at a state-of-the-art facility somewhere out there.

I got it out though, and once I figured out how to get the antifreeze to flow only through the trailer's plumbing system, and to stop flowing onto the driveway, I was able to move to the next step of getting the cover onto the trailer. That was a lot easier said than done.

Without an attached ladder to climb up onto the top, I was forced to get creative with the covering technique. Between my wife and I, we took the better part of two hours to do a 20-minute job (as my neighbour so kindly demonstrated a week later). But, at the end of the day, we had a nicely winterized and covered trailer that was all set up to ride out the winter. And best of all, it had taken me so long to get this done that now it was too late to rake the leaves.

Oh darn! That's so sad!

"Oh well, I guess I'll just have to do that later in the week", I thought with a grin.

But my joy was bound to be short-lived. As the night wore on, there arose a windstorm that was nothing short of hair-raising. Winds were gusting upwards of 40km/hr, rattling windows and snapping tree branches. We could sit in the den and listen to the flapping of the trailer cover all night. I was sure I had strapped the cover down properly, but the way things were sounding outside I was half-prepared to go outside and find the trailer floating through the air not unlike a hot air balloon. I couldn't see the trailer pad from our bedroom window, but I could see the silhouette of surrounding trees swaying in the pitch-black backyard and I just hoped that nothing would go flying in the wrong direction and force me to have to make an insurance claim.

I barely slept that night because of how loud and strong the wind was.

The next morning I got up, got the kids squared away, then headed out to inspect the damage. I cautiously went out the front door of the house, heading to the side of the house where the RV was parked. The trailer was still there, as was the cover (thankfully), but it was obvious that it had been a rough night. The zippers had been undone, the straps had wiggled loose, some parts were hanging off while others were barely hanging on – my previous day's efforts had been all but nullified.

I was not amused.

Then I rounded the side of the house and got a glimpse of the backyard.

My lusciously green lawn was staring back at me – it had reappeared. The leaves and twigs that were the bane of my existence yesterday were now piled up, almost neatly, against the fence in one corner of the backyard. And not only had the backyard been cleared, the limbs of the trees were also bare. The wind did a real number on my RV cover, but it did me a real favor with the backyard.

My only conundrum at this point was whether to share this happening with Sophon, or to just take the credit for raking the backyard in record time. Hmmm…….

There are very few things in life that happen in isolation, and that is a truth that is most often realized in hindsight. In the moment of a challenge or a triumph, the focus tends to be placed on what is going on and how it affects one's present reality. Very rarely is there any thought given to the happenings that might counterbalance a particular occurrence.

There is the popular saying that goes, "for everything you win there's something lost". While that simple statement is packed with wisdom and truth, the converse is also true – we seldom lose something without gaining something else. The windstorm that wreaked havoc on my brand new RV cover saved me the grunt work of raking the leaves, and had I stopped investigating when I saw the ravaged polypropylene material half-strewn across the lawn at the side of the house, I would have missed the gift that was waiting in the backyard.

I've found that it is important for me to take the time to be critical of things that happen in my life. I jump at any chance to celebrate my wins, but I always seek to identify what those wins might have cost. When things don't go as I would like, I mourn my losses, but search for the opportunities and blessings that accompany those losses. I have found that things are rarely what they seem initially, and the whole story is seldom told in a single sentence.

"….*our God turned the curse into a blessing*" – Nehemiah 13:2

Postlude

There is a saying that goes, "life is 10% what happens to you and 90% how you react to it". You have undoubtedly come across variations of that anecdote with the attributed percentages changing based on context, source, and/or desired impact. Regardless of the different ways that the sentiment is expressed, the underlying principle remains very, very true. It is our attitude towards the happenings in life that decide the quality of life that we will have. Life happens, and it will always just *happen*! There is no controlling it, nor is there any choosing of what our overall experience will be. Any hope of selecting what will or will not come our way is severely misplaced and should be decidedly discarded. When it comes to navigating life's occurrences, our only power lies in how we choose to interpret the occurrences, and the impact we allow them to have on us.

By way of my upbringing, combined with my personal choice and chosen professional path, I seek to find the opportunity for growth and learning in every triggering occurrence. Now, I will not be foolhardy and declare that there is a lesson in the bite of every mosquito that you have ever received (though there very well might be). What I will state instead is that if an occurrence triggers a deep-seated reaction within you, then there is a high likelihood that an opportunity for personal growth is present.

Developing the disposition to see these opportunities, however, takes time and deliberate effort. Coming to the recognition that we are all students in the school of life where graduates are given obituaries, not diplomas, allows for the acceptance of lessons as they come.

In recent years, many educational institutions have embarked on initiatives that are meant to make learning more flexible and accessible for their learners. The reimagining of what teaching and learning could be, brought on by the COVID-19 pandemic, now has people questioning the rigidity that was present in classrooms for so long. Well, life's classroom has always been accessible, flexible, diverse and inclusive. It is up to us, the learners, to accept the teaching that is being offered.

Lessons for life are contained within everyday experiences!

www.ingramcontent.com/pod-product-compliance
Lightning Source LLC
LaVergne TN
LVHW010108170826
845678LV00012B/2293